GARDENING FOR FRAGRANCE

GARDENING
FOR
FRAGRANCE

ANN
BONAR

WARD LOCK

ACKNOWLEDGEMENTS

The publishers are grateful to the following for granting permission
to reproduce the colour photographs: Harry Smith Horticultural
Photographic Collection (pp 32, 35, 45, 46, 58, 61, 62, 72, 73, 75, 77,
82, 92 (both), 95 (above), & 101 (below); Pat Brindley (pp 2, 7, 29,
42, 51, 68 (below), 88, 96 & 105); Photos Horticultural Picture Library
(pp 14, 27, 43, 59, 85, 93 (both), 95 (below), 101 (above), 107 & 111);
and Ann Bonar (pp 39, 55 & 68 (above).

All the line drawings, except those in Chapter 1, are by Mike
Shoebridge.

First published in Great Britain in 1990
by Ward Lock Limited, Villiers House,
41/47 Strand, London WC2N 5JE, England
A Cassell Imprint

House editor Denis Ingram

Text filmset in Linotype Garamond Original
by Tradespools Ltd, Frome, Somerset
Printed and bound in Yugoslavia
by Papirografika

British Library Cataloguing in Publication Data
Bonar, Ann
Gardening for fragrance.
1. Gardens. Scented plants
I. Title
635.968

ISBN 0 7063 6900 9

CONTENTS

Preface   6

Chapter One
Fragrance and aroma in plants   8

Chapter Two
Scented plants in history   18

Chapter Three
Cottage garden flowers in spring   26

Chapter Four
High summer in the cottage garden   38

Chapter Five
Fragrant boskage   54

Chapter Six
The Rosarie   80

Chapter Seven
Herbal fragrance and aroma   98

Chapter Eight
Scented lawns and groundcovers   112

Chapter Nine
Plant growth and health   118
Index   126

PREFACE

The collection of plants that makes up a garden is more of a wide-ranging personal statement by the owner than almost anything else. One is free, in a garden, to indulge one's eyes (and ears), one's sense of taste and touch, curiosity, physical ability, learning, dexterity, activity—or not—and last, but certainly not least, sense of smell.

The garden's existence at all is justified primarily on two counts: to provide beauty, and to supply food. Both are furnished by plants, and beauty is increased by the presence of fragrance and aroma; flowers in particular are much more charming when scented – however beautiful a flower is in shape and colour, it is somehow sterile without perfume.

A flower with fragrance has a complete effect, appealing to taste—the end product of smell—as well as sight. A flower without perfume has no soul; witness the many beautiful flowers which, when automatically sniffed are found, unhappily, to lack this last quality.

A garden alive with fragrances and aromas has a fourth dimension. Aromas are just as beguiling as fragrance, and just as heady. They are mostly contained in leaves, so that gardening for aroma can lead to the planting of many new plants which would not otherwise have been considered, because their appearance was not striking. The choice of flowers, too, is likely to be increased, to include those with pale-coloured blooms and a delicate and ephemeral appeal. Their positioning is all the more crucial, to make the most of their looks. Such flowering plants often have the strongest fragrances, especially at dusk, and placing these beneath windows ensures that they scent the home as well as the garden.

However, there are hundreds of beautiful garden plants which are scented or aromatic, and there is no reason why the garden should not be fragrant all year round—winter-flowering plants are often scented. Fragrances can follow one another or overlap; they can mingle, contrast or blend. Flowery, fruity and spicy fragrances are all contained in flowers, including delectable food smells like that of chocolate; aromas add a sharp note to contrast the essential character of fragrance and lend it pungency.

Above all, fragrance induces a sense of tranquillity and peace. Such gardens are always places in which to relax and take time slowly; burgeoning weeds can be forgotten, and even forgiven if they are scented.

A.B.

The yellow and mahogany coloured wallflowers have the strongest perfume, though all are scented to some degree.

CHAPTER ONE

FRAGRANCE AND AROMA IN PLANTS

There is nothing more evocative of places and people, experiences and atmospheres than perfume, except perhaps music. The fragrance of jasmine calls up hot tropical nights, the scent of honeysuckle evokes memories of English gardens on a summer evening, and the aromatic smell of a bed of thyme under a baking sun instantly recalls a Mediterranean landscape of parched rocks and hillsides.

Fragrance adds a fourth dimension to a plant, a tantalizing one, because it is invisible and elusive—the harder and longer you sniff, the more it disperses. The perfume of a rose like 'Wendy Cussons', caught as you pass by, forces you to stop and go back to enjoy it for longer, as you bury your nose in a bloom. Disappointingly, more is not better; doubtless a gentle rebuke for being greedy.

Nevertheless, the fragrance of plants is powerful and varied: it is mostly emitted by their flowers, with leaves coming a close second, and some have scented roots or aromatic bark and seeds. Why are not all plants aromatic in some way? Does aroma play a definite part in a plant's life cycle; is it of positive use to them? The answer to this question is yes. There are two main reasons for its presence: fragrance in flowers attracts pollinating insects, and the aromas of leaves help to protect the plant from the desiccating effects of heat.

POLLINATION

Flowers which are self-fertile, not needing the pollen from another flower or another plant of the same genus, are practically never scented. If cross-fertilization is required, a plant ensures this by a variety of methods, such as wind, water, birds, insects etc. Wind and water pollination are primitive methods, but bird and insect pollination are more sophisticated, often requiring a modification of the flower itself. One of the main modifications has been the development of fragrance to attract insects; when birds are involved with pollination, by feeding on the nectar of flowers, they are attracted by colours.

There is an association between colour and flower perfume which is an interesting one: the more coloured the flowers are, the less perfume is present. This is because the perfume originates from chlorophyll which is present in petals as well as in leaves, where it appears as the green pigment. The more the chlorophyll is modified to produce aroma, the more likely is the flower to be white, pale yellow, pink, lilac-pink or purple. If the chlorophyll is not changed into aroma, it will be converted to a variety of strongly coloured pigments, with the result that red, orange and blue flowers are rarely scented. Flowers which are blue or deep yellow are pollinated by bees, which use sight to guide them to the nectar they require; red and green look the same to them, so they naturally home in on the alternatives. Birds, on the other hand, see blue and green as the same colour, so make for the brilliant red and orange flowers.

However, if fragrance is the attractant, flower colouring will be on the pale side, lilac, purple or mauve, cream, yellow, white or white tinged with pink or lilac. That is not to say that all fragrant flowers are wishy-washy in colour; some of the most fragrant of the old shrub roses are intensely and strikingly coloured in shades of crimson, rose, deep wine and purple. There is a deep golden-yellow daylily (*Hemorocallis lutea*) which is delightfully scented; a fragrant blue and yellow species gladiolus (*G. recurvus*); and the evening primrose (*Oenothera biennis*) is a classic example of a bright yellow flower which is perfumed. Wallflowers, too, have a delicious perfume. Conversely, there are plenty of white flowers which lack an aroma: daisies, campanulas, some white roses and even some of the mock orange blossom hybrids are unscented. Many of the primarily purple and pink petunias, cyclamen and clematis have no fragrance.

Insects see colour quite differently from us, however; because they can see by ultraviolet light, white is not necessarily white to them, and a collection of white flowers can, to their eyes, consist of a mixture of colours.

If a flower is fragrant its pollinators are likely to be butterflies and moths, because in such flowers the nectar is secreted deep inside the flower, and it is only these insects, with their long tongues, which can reach the nectar. In some cases, fragrance is only present to stimulate the insect to go through the motions which ensure pollination.

Since bees rely on their sight to a large extent it is not only overall colour which is an important signal to them. They also look for markings on flowers to guide them to the nectar, so that flowers with spotted or veined throats, like foxgloves, are unlikely to be scented. Few blue flowers are fragrant, hyacinths and iris being exceptions; many of these unscented blue flowers have bell-shaped blooms and make up the families of borage, campanulas and labiates such as bugle and meadow clary.

Butterflies are diurnal insects, moths usually nocturnal, and if the evening and night-flowering plants are moth-pollinated, their flowers are likely to be white or pale coloured. Such plants naturally grow in positions which receive some shade during the day, and light woodland is a source of many plants with fragrant flowers.

In the daytime it will be butterflies which are visiting flowers for their nectar, so growing fragrant flowers will automatically make the garden a more colourful place; it will encourage a better mixture of wild life in general, as well as help to maintain species of Lepidoptera. You will encourage beetles, too, to live in the garden if you grow plants whose flowers have a fruity scent, such as magnolias, allspice (calycanthus) and Spanish gorse (*Genista hispanica*).

PROTECTION

I said earlier that scent had two functions: pollination is one; the other is protection. Where it is protective, it can be better defined as aroma; the odour is of a different quality altogether, much more pungent, powerful and hardly sweet at all. Rather, it is spicy, nose-tickling and sometimes even bitter. Aromas occur mainly in leaves and often only contain one constituent, the essential oil itself, such as eucalyptol from eucalyptus; this makes them more intense and lingering than flower essences.

Plants with aromatic leaves are generally found naturally in hot climates, and have adapted to the high temperatures, in the same way that cacti have adapted to deserts and heat by developing a round plant body from which the least water can be transpired. Essential oils have taken the place of water to some degree in the leaves, and are nowhere near so readily transpired under intense sunlight as water, though anyone who has walked on a sunny Italian hillside will know that some oil becomes airborne and fills the atmosphere. When they do escape from the leaves, they form a protective veil of oil vapour above the leaf for much longer than water vapour would. A good example of this is the burning bush, *Dictamnus albus*, a herbaceous perennial from eastern Europe. If a lighted match is put in the air above its leaves on a hot day, the air bursts into flame! The essential oil in this plant is very volatile and easily vaporized, and it is also very inflammable; its aroma is of lemon and balsam when the leaves are bruised or crushed.

Hence an aromatic leaf survives heat and drought much more easily than an odourless one, and this explains why so many foliage plants of this type are found in hot dry places: cistus species, pelargoniums from South Africa, lemon verbena and eucalyptus from Australia. The smell of the aroma does not appear to act as an attractant to insects or animals, but it is possible that, besides helping to keep the plant moist in a dry environment, essential oils actually function as repellants for any creatures which might attempt to feed on leaves and stems. Further, these oils often have antiseptic properties, such as those contained in thyme and rosemary, and perhaps they help to keep the plants free from fungal or bacterial disease as well. Certainly, aromatic plants rarely suffer from ill-health, and those with scented flowers often seem to be free from insect attack. Maybe plant breeders should investigate this aspect more thoroughly, in view of the current distaste for the use of chemical pesticides.

SUBSTANCE OF ODOUR

All parts of a plant can produce fragrance or aroma, not only the flowers and leaves, but also the bark, the roots, buds, stems, seeds and seed-pods (for example, the pods of vanilla) and fruits, which have their own distinctive aromas. The plant cells which contain any kind of odour, including offensive ones, may be gathered together to form glands or hairs which release their scents when exposed to heat or broken by crushing in some way.

The scented oil of flowers will be found mainly in the outermost cells of the upper and lower surfaces of the petals; if sepals or bracts have replaced the petals, the oil will be found there instead.

Technically, the fragrances and aromas of essential oils are mostly terpenes, and the aromas of peppermint, lemon, rose and lavender come from oils which largely consist of these terpenes. They are not at all the same, chemically speaking, as fats and oils such as linseed or sunflower oil. Other substances are also nearly always present in any particular oil; for instance, the essential oil of rose contains at least eight, and each substance may be in different parts of the petal or sepal which can, accordingly be coloured differently. Until the oil is needed by the plant, it fills the relevant plant cells, taking the place of the normal cell contents, and is stored there as a glucoside, i.e. combined with sugar, until required. It is only when fermentation has started, or what is in fact decay, that the perfume of the oil is released. Opening of the flower has to occur first, so that oxygen from the air may be taken in and oxidation of the oil begin; even then, it may not be fragrant at once. Once open, the oil is released continuously until the flower fades—in effect it is a waste product.

There must be other reasons for the presence of scent in flowers besides these suggestions, however, since flowers with thin petals are practically always unscented; it is those with thick, or comparatively thick, petals which contain fragrance. One reason may be for the cooling effect that is a property of aromatic oils, but in that case thin petals should also be scented.

PERFUME GROUPS

There appears to be a bewildering range of perfumes and aromas scattered throughout the plant kingdom, but in fact flower fragrances have been classified into only 10 groups, and leaf aromas into only four, although some leaves produce aromas which fit better into the flower groups. Particular plant families account for scents as well: examples are the *Pinaceae*, *Myrtaceae*, *Lauraceae*, *Labiatae* and the *Umbelliferae*. Scent is by no means spread across the complete range of plant families, although any type of plant may be aromatic or fragrant, whether it is a herbaceous perennial, a bulb, a tree or a fungus. The most familiar perfumes are those of the rose, lily, violet, jasmine and carnation; most well-known aromas are balsam, camphor, menthol, eucalyptus and peppermint.

Flower perfume groups
Rose group　The fragrance of the rose flower can be found in other flowers as well, such as peonies and *Iris hoogiana*, a beautiful grey-blue iris which flowers in late spring and comes from Turkestan. It is also found in parts of the plant other than the flower, for instance leaves such as those found on *Pelargonium capitatum*, which is one of the scented-leaved geraniums, and roots, such as in *Rhodiola rosea* (syn. *Sedum rhodiola*), whose dried roots smell so strongly of roses that the plant is commonly called rose-root. The perfume of roses themselves is not completely pure, and often has overtones of other scents or even spicy and fruity aromas. Nevertheless, it is one of the most refreshing and sweet of all the perfumes. Although perfume is present in some of the roses, they are not pollinated by butterflies, because there is no nectar, and they rely instead on beetles.
Violet group　In this group the fragrance of the flowers is due to a ketone called ionone; in roots which are violet-scented, it is due to another called irone. *Viola odorata* has a beautiful perfume and its white counterpart is even more strongly scented; *Iris reticulata* smells of violets, and so does *Crinum × powellii* and *Gladiolus recurvus*. Orris root is used in perfumery to supply the violet fragrance; it is the dried rhizome of *Iris* 'Florentina'. Interestingly, some violets, like roses, do not need butterflies to pollinate them, or indeed any insects: some species with flowers, such as *V. odorata*, are pollinated by bees, others have under-developed petals, which never open, so that self-fertilization occurs. *V. odorata* can produce this second type of flower as well, later in the year, after its main flush.
Aromatic group　In spite of its name, this group does contain many scented flowers, whose perfume has a spicy tang to it—it is not entirely sweet. So many

of them, however, contain other perfumes, that classification into groups is not always satisfactory. Some could quite well be placed in two groups; for instance some roses contain both the almond scent, which is included here, and the violet perfume. Besides almond, other odours which are pleasantly aromatic are: vanilla, often associated with lemon, as in witch-hazel (*Hamamelis mollis*), *Clematis montana, Laburnum × watereri* 'Vossii' and sweetpea. The almond previously mentioned is found in *Choisya ternata* (Mexican orange blossom); heliotrope, in which it is very pronounced, and flowering rushes. Clove, due to the presence of eugenol, is found a little in peonies, much more in *Silene noctiflora* (night-scented catchfly), and of course, stocks, carnations and pinks. The tropical clove tree itself, *Eugenia aromatica*, is the most renowned source of this aroma, and cinnamon (*Cinnamomum zeylanica*) also contains it, but in both of these the aroma is in the leaves and bark. Aniseed is a fourth in this group, found in cowslips, magnolias and *Illicium anisatum*, the star anise, and balsam is the essential fragrance of hyacinths and night-scented stock. It is notable how many of the flowers in this group are white, yellow or pink, though it does contain a few of the rarely scented blue flowers.

Lemon group   The sharp refreshing aroma of lemon is mostly found in leaves, but some flowers do contain it, often associated with other scents, as, for instance, verbena, *Magnolia × soulangeana*, the evening primrose (*Oenothera biennis*) and *Rosa bracteata*, a climbing rose from China with large, white, single flowers in midsummer. Pollination of this group is by beetles.

Heavy group   As would be expected, this contains flowers which are exceptionally strongly scented, for instance *Lilium candidum*, lilac, philadelphus (syringa), jonquils and *Hemerocallis lutea*, the golden daylily. Even honeysuckle and lily-of-the-valley form part of this group. Most are pollinated by moths, and many are woodland plants from sub-tropical regions such as the centre of China and South America. Indole forms part of the essential oil, together with benzylacetate and methyl anthranilate, and is the ingredient which makes the smell unpleasant when inhaled close to; it is reminiscent of decomposition. Practically all the flowers in this group are pale in colour, white, pale yellow, cream or pastel pink.

Fruit-scented group   The fragrances in this group are considerably varied; it does not include lemon, but there are, for instance, pineapple (*Cytisus battandieri*); plums (*Muscari racemosum*, grape hyacinth); apricot (*Iris graminea*), and many of the roses include fruity overtones such as apple, orange and banana (see pp. 80 and 89).

Honey group   The scent of these flowers is light and delicate, but quite definitely present, and with a sweeter overtone than is found in the equally delicate fragrance of primroses which are part of the aromatic group. The leading example of this group has to be the buddleia, also called the butterfly bush, whose spikes of flowers attract a mass of butterflies—tortoiseshells, red admirals and peacocks—in late summer and autumn. Scabious and sweet sultan (*Centaurea moschata*), honeysuckle and *Sedum spectabile* are other flowering plants with the same sweet honey smell, and all are butterfly plants, too.

These seven groups form the most pleasant-smelling of the ten in the classification; the remaining three are unpleasant, so need not be considered in detail. They consist of the *indoloid, aminoid* and *animal-scented* groups, and are largely pollinated by flies. The indoloid group contains many plants from the tropical countries of south-east Asia and South America, with brownish flowers, often smelling of putrefying meat. The aminoid plants have a fishy ammonia smell in their white or creamy flowers—amelanchier, privet and pyracantha are examples, although the smell of privet flowers in the air is pleasantly sweet to my nostrils. The garlic odour is another example.

Animal-scented flowers often have a fruity aroma as well as the predominant animal one, and can be pleasant when the flowers have just opened; *Fritillaria imperialis* is said to have a foxy smell, and the flowering currant (*Ribes roseum*) is distinctly reminiscent of tom-cats. The smell of musk comes from some animals, and makes a link between this group and the honey-scented group; *Rosa moschata* is an example, so also is *Muscari muscarimi*. Plants with musk-scented flowers mostly come from the mountains between Afghanistan and China.

Leaf aroma groups
Leaves can contain flower perfumes as well as their own aromas, which are much more pungent and penetrating, and mostly not found in flowers. Rosemary, for instance, has a particularly refreshing and nose-tickling smell when its leaves are crushed, and so has eucalyptus. Most aromatic leaves retain their aroma when dry, and indeed it is actually stronger, because the water has evaporated, thus concentrating the essential oil. All the flower perfumes are represented in leaves, surprisingly; one of the most unexpected is the rose perfume, which occurs in the scented-leaved pelargoniums, such as *P. denticulatum*, *P. graveolens* and *P. radula*, where it is actually much purer than in rose flowers.

Mint group   In this group there are all the species and varieties of mint, some of which add strong overtones of fruits to the minty (menthol) smell, such as apple, orange and pineapple; some of the scented-leaved pelargoniums can be included here as well, together with eucalyptus, which contains menthol, but not as its chief ingredient.

Camphor and eucalyptus group   Here there is a great variety of plants, many of them herbs, such as sage, catmint, chamomile, sweet bay and the camphor plant, *Balsamita major*. The Carolina allspice (*Calycanthus floridus*) is another example in which these aromas are present in all parts of the plant, though the fruity smell of the petals overlies it in the flowers. Rosemary, myrtle, lavender and *Pelargonium* 'Clorinda' are counted here, too.

Sulphur group   Almost any sulphur compound has an unpleasant smell; for example hydrogen sulphide smells of bad eggs. They only occur, however, in roots and leaves of, for instance, onions, watercress, and particularly garlic.

Turpentine group   This is the smallest of the leaf groups, of which rosemary is an example, containing borneol acetate.

Aromatic bark groups
The bark of many trees and shrubs can also have a strong smell; there are only two groups: the aromatic and the turpentine.

The former contains *Magnolia × soulangeana*, with bark smelling of lemon; *Drimys winteri*, the winter's bark, is renowned for its aromatic bark, as is the bark of the cinnamon tree, *Cinnamomum zeylanica*. In the turpentine group is the small tree from which Chian turpentine was originally obtained, *Pistacio terebinthus*, from the Mediterranean. The group also includes *Pinus palustris* and *P. pinaster*, American and European pines respectively, which are sources of ordinary turpentine. Some of the cedars and the blue spruce (*Picea pungens* Glauca group) belong here, too.

SCENT EXTRACTION

While it is delightful to smell and enjoy the fragrance of flowers, it is even nicer to smell delicious oneself, and as long ago as 3500 BC the Egyptians had learnt the art of extracting perfume, mostly with the aid of an oil, itself obtained from a plant such as the almond or the olive, and of fixing it so that it did not quickly evaporate. Its permanency was of such a degree that when Tutankhamun's tomb was opened in 1922, there were substances in some of the containers which were still fragrant—Tutankhamun was alive in 1350 BC.

The Greeks and Romans valued perfume highly and used it a great deal in all sorts of ways, but it was the Arabs in the tenth century who did some organized research into the method of extraction which involves distillation, still one of the chief methods of obtaining perfume. There are several other techniques, all with advantages and disadvantages, which have been modified and streamlined in the light of modern information and experience.

Enfleurage

This is a technique which can be adapted from old professional methods so that it can be used at home. The principle was to use freshly gathered flowers pressed tightly between thin layers of fat so that the perfume cells were broken and the essential oil escaped, to be absorbed by the fat. Sheets of perfectly clean glass in frames were used, and melted animal fat spread on both surfaces; then the glass sheets were stacked up 20 thick, and the flowers left in position for 24 hours, to be replaced by a fresh layer. This went on for a month, after which the fat was removed and treated with alcohol to extract the essential perfume oil.

At home it is possible to do this with olive oil, filling the oil with fresh flowers and changing them as above, until the oil smells very strongly of the perfume. Then add an equal amount of pure alcohol, shake well and leave for two–four weeks, shaking vigorously every day. Pour off the alcohol, which will have absorbed the fragrant oil, bottle firmly and keep in a cool dark place.

Distillation

There are two methods used here: boiling water and steam. If boiling water is used, the flowers are mixed with it and the essential oil will then vaporize and mix with the steam. By cooling the steam so that it condenses and becomes water again, the oil is also condensed and will float on the surface of the cool water, when it can be drawn off. Where steam is used, the flowers are put into a large container, and steam passed through them from the base, collected and cooled, and then treated in the same way. The water itself—the distillate—will also be fragrant and is of value, but one of the drawbacks is that only flowers which can stand a good deal of heat can be used, so that it tends to be confined to roses and orange-blossom.

Extraction

This is a less injurious method and can result in a purer form of the perfume; it is used for such flowers as orange-blossom, mimosa, jonquil and carnation. A volatile solvent, generally petroleum ether, is allowed to wash repeatedly through

Opposite:
The eucalyptus, as the Eucalyptus gunnii *shown here, has extremely aromatic foliage, which is very refreshing when crushed.*

Fig. 1 *An alembic used in the seventeenth century for distilling essential oil; all joints were hermetically sealed.*

tiers of perforated metal plates on which are layers of flowers, contained in an air-tight vessel, until the solvent is saturated with the essential oil. The solvent is then drawn into a still and heated to evaporation point, the residue being a soft wax-like material containing the essential fragrant oil. The wax is a natural material contained in the flowers, unavoidably affected by the solvent, and the whole is known as 'floral concrete'. By treating this in turn with alcohol, the precious oil is dissolved into the alcohol, which is distilled, leaving at last the oil, known as the 'floral absolute'. This is an extremely concentrated form of the flower perfume, exceptionally pure, and when diluted to the right degree, will exactly reproduce the perfume concerned. It is also extremely expensive.

Another method of extraction is called *maceration*, whereby the flowers are put into hot oil or fat, and fresh batches of flowers added to the oil daily until it is fully charged with perfume.

Expression

This is probably the simplest method, but it is not used for flowers, only for seeds and fruits, and particularly nowadays to obtain the oil from such seeds as those of sunflower and mustard, and from fruits such as the olive. For perfumery, only the citrus fruits are suitable—orange, lemon, bergamot and mandarin. Quite simply, the peel from these fruits is crushed between rollers and the resulting pulp centrifuged to separate out the oil.

CHAPTER TWO

SCENTED PLANTS IN HISTORY

The word paradise is derived via the Greeks from the ancient Persian word *pardes*, which literally means hunting ground or park. Wherever the Persians went they created gardens; but gardens were not their invention—they copied the idea from the Babylonians and Assyrians. Our records of gardens, however, trace their creation even further back, to the ancient Egyptians, who went in for gardening in a surprisingly big way, considering their climate and the tiny amount of land that contained fertile soil and water—the Sahara was after all, even then, on their back doorstep.

There are detailed records of the plans of Egyptian gardens of about 2000 BC, and, in an account of a garden in existence in about 1520 BC belonging to a builder to the king of the time, Tuthmosis I, a variety of trees and shrubs is listed, one of which is myrtle, a plant native to western Asia.

The Indians cultivated gardens, too, and even further east still, the great Chinese civilizations must have had gardens, though their records do not appear to extend further back than about 500 BC, and then the reference is only an indirect one, when Confucius mentioned that perfumed flowers were used at festivals.

In all the gardens of these civilizations it seems that plants with fragrance or aroma were grown as a matter of course, because scented parts of plants were used in religious rites and ceremonies. The smell of burning incense is well known for inducing altered mental and emotional states, and even today the sacred fire which burns at Hindu marriages is kept alight with scented oils.

THE EARLIEST AROMAS

One wonders what civilization would have done if all these aromas and fragrances had not been available in the plants growing so abundantly round them? It is remarkable how many plants there are in the area, for example, from Egypt through Syria and Saudi Arabia to Iran (Persia) and northern India, which have an odour of some kind. One reason could be concerned with the hot climate, since aromatic oils serve to protect plants from drying out better than water does.

To start with, myrrh was the most prized aromatic. It is a golden resin obtained from the trunk of a small tree, sometimes a large shrub, *Commiphora myrrha*, native to Somali, Yemen and Arabia; for many hundreds of years it was practically the only substance known to provide a lasting perfume. Along with myrrh went frankincense, another resin from an evergreen tree, *Boswellia carteri*, also from south Arabia and Somali, and both travelled along a route known as the Incense Road, in the same way that Chinese silk found its way to the outside world via a route called the Silk Road.

They were carried by camel and donkey from the south to the north for use in the festivities and religious rites of the temples of the time, and this trade went on peacefully for nearly 2000 years, until the time of Solomon. Then the cargo had to travel through Israeli lands; Israel was unfriendly to the countries of the south, and so the Queen of Sheba, who ruled southern Arabia, was forced to use a good deal of diplomacy and intelligence, not to say her beauty, to ensure that the trade on which her country depended, could continue.

Another aromatic much used was balm of Gilead, *Commiphora opobalsamum*, a small evergreen tree with three-parted leaves and white flowers in threes; the scented material is obtained as resin from the trunk, and by expression from the unripe berries. It is similarly native of the south of Arabia, Yemen and surrounding regions, and should not be confused with *Cedronella triphylla*, another balm of Gilead, indigenous to the Canary Islands. This is quite a different plant, being a rather soft stemmed shrub about 1.2 m (4 ft) tall; its leaves have a particularly powerful aroma (see p. 103). Spikenard was a fourth plant valued for its perfume, obtained from the short thick roots. *Nardostachys jatamansii* comes from India, and is hardy; it has pale rose-purple flowers and grows 30 cm (12 in) tall.

Thyme, southernwood, peppermint and marjoram were other plants whose aromatic leaves were commonly used, plants which are still in use today in Europe as herbs for cooking and household needs. The Madonna lily, *Lilium candidum*, was twined into wreaths worn on the head by guests at banquets, as was the lotus, *Nelumbo nucifera*. This aquatic plant, related to the waterlily, has extremely fragrant white flowers, tipped with pink or rose. Although air conditioning was not part of everyday life, when swags of aromatic leaves were hung on the walls at such feasts, their sharp odours were refreshing and cooling.

THE EGYPTIANS

The Egyptians had an elaborate and intricate system of religion, and a variety of aromas and fragrances were used by their priests for burning in the temples. For instance, a mixture called *kyphi* contained myrrh, scented rushes, resin and juniper berries; sometimes cinnamon, mint and frankincense were included, since there were different versions of the mixture, probably depending on the priest concerned and what he considered to be suitable for the purpose.

As the Egyptian civilization progressed, refinement set in, not least in the area of personal hygiene; in a country where the temperature is always high, the Egyptians extended their use and knowledge of perfumes to their own bodies, mostly in the form of fragrant ointments and anointing oils.

The art of making up these mixtures became highly sophisticated, and was largely in the hands of the priests. One that was particularly popular contained the lily perfume, but it must have been very expensive and only used by women from wealthy families. Its preparation certainly took at least a week, and involved such ingredients as oil, lily petals, myrrh, cardamom, honey, salt, cinnamon and crocus, all of which were strained, bruised, beaten, sieved and skimmed, by hand, until the end product was finally stored in small pots made of alabaster coated inside with gum, saffron and honey mixed with water.

Cleopatra herself (69–30 BC) is said to have soaked the purple sails of her barge in perfume when she met Mark Antony for the first time. By that date perfume was considered essential to everyday use by the upper classes, and was also frequently part of middle class life, though not to the same extent.

Scented fat was a third method of perfuming the body, but not a pleasant one to modern eyes. A cone of fat previously mixed with spices and herbs was put on the top of the head, or on the wig if worn, when a party or some sort of festivity was in progress. In due course this melted so that, as it ran down the body, one's clothes and skin became saturated with its perfume.

Aromas and fragrances were also used by the Egyptians when embalming the bodies of royalty and other members of the upper classes. The coffin might be made of a scented wood such as cedar, and the body wrapped in linen cloth treated with fragrant resin, while the body itself was injected with perfumed oils such as cassia and myrrh. All this care was taken because the Egyptians believed in existence after death for which the dead person had to be prepared.

THE PERSIANS

Egypt and its civilization lasted for well over 3000 years, and its culture and life style permeated the whole of the Near and Middle East, but inevitably in time it began to crumble. Persia became a mighty force, but in turn was overthrown by the Greeks, under the regime of Alexander, who systematically invaded countries to the east until they reached India. In spite of all this fighting, there was still time to pick up the customs of the conquered country, and the use of fragrant roses that the Persians so enjoyed was one of their contributions to everyday living. Many scented roses grow wild in what is now called Iran (Persia), Syria and surrounding regions—*Rosa damascena* is a native and so is the red rose, *R. gallica*, whose variety *officinalis* is so much concerned in making perfume.

The Persians and the Hebrews carried on the widespread use of aromatic odours as the Egyptians did, and the Persians in particular developed the art of gardening as well, to a much greater extent than the Egyptians, growing scented plants of their own in their gardens.

THE GREEKS

As the Greeks became dominant, gardens as such became much less evident, but they lifted the art of using perfumes and aromatics to a degree of holiness, for the use of the gods alone. However, they must have overcome this view at some point since, in one of the classical poems by Antiphanes, one of the wealthier Greeks is described as using a variety of perfumes when bathing: mint extract on arms, marjoram on hair, thyme on neck and knees, and feet and legs were massaged in 'rich Egyptian unguents'.

The use of aromas and perfumes seems to mark a certain stage of advancement in the development of a civilization; they both figure largely throughout the east, from Egypt as far east as India, where their part in religion was and is still widespread. Incense was burned, roses and jasmine were used to make perfume, and sandalwood was mixed with camphor, turmeric and other aromatic sources to provide a powder for household use.

The Greeks used scented oils on their heads, as the Egyptians did, but for a more definite purpose, as such oils were thought to help the general health if applied as near the brain as possible. Guests were offered aromatherapy after a bath when they first arrived, and even wine was perfumed, the best being produced at Byblos. By this time, perfumes were as much in evidence as aromas, and had many more personal applications than aromas. As their qualities were discovered, so perfumes became more and more popular, but they were still expensive and were the prerogative of the middle and upper classes.

THE ROMANS

In early Roman times scents and aromas were virtually unused; it was only as time went on that the Greek tradition of using perfumes in everyday life began to insinuate itself into the Roman life style. Indeed, Caesar thought their use by anyone to be effeminate, and the sale of perfumes of any kind in any form was forbidden in 188 BC. However, as the Roman armies progressed down the Italian peninsula to the south, and marched east through today's Balkans, they met out-lying clusters of Greek settlers, and from them picked up the habit of perfumery. Its use increased rapidly as the Empire matured, so bearing out the idea of perfume being part of a developed culture.

Eventually the Romans became infatuated with it, so that perfume was used by everyone, including the Roman army, whose standards were coated with perfumed ointments on national holidays. They even fought with wreaths of roses on their helmets, and returned from victories with roses on their chariots.

Roses were one of their great sources of perfumes, and the petals were used to carpet the floor at dinner parties; not only that, they were showered down on to the guests from the ceiling, and it is said that at one of these festivities some of the guests were suffocated, the mass of petals was so great. Nero slept on them and is said to have complained of insomnia if one petal was curled!

Besides roses, the *saffron* crocus was of major importance and rivalled the rose in its popularity. *Crocus sativus* has lilac and purple blooms, centred with prominent, brilliant orange-red stigmas, the source of its fragrance; it flowers in the autumn. It needs warmth and good drainage to grow well and increase so, not surprisingly, it is found growing wild from Italy to India. Since the time of Solomon, when saffron was called *karkon*, it has been grown commercially.

In spite of the fact that nearly 100 000 flowers were needed to produce one pound of saffron taken from the stigmas, it was added to fountains on festival days in Rome, and scattered from the roof of the amphitheatre at the Games. Nowadays it is used for flavouring food, and is still extremely expensive.

Fragrances and aromas could be obtained made up in three different ways: as *powders*, as rather thick *liquids* with oil bases, and as *ointments*. Our modern bath talc must be a derivative of the Roman *powder*, but the latter was used, not directly on the body, but for perfuming clothing and linen, and might contain orris root, labdanum, spikenard and cinnamon. Labdanum is the aromatic gum exuded by two species of the rock rose, *Cistus* × *cyprius* and *C. incanus creticus*.

The *liquids* contained fixative oils, such as olive oil or oil of ben, an oil obtained from the seeds of the small tree *Moringa aptera*, native to Egypt, Syria and Arabia, and to these oils was added a mixture of perfumes and aromas: marjoram, lily, myrrh, cinnamon and saffron. The *solid* unguents usually contained only single perfumes or aromas such as rose, or that obtained from *Cyperus rotundus*, a sedge with aromatic rhizomes.

EUROPEAN MIDDLE AGES

When the Roman empire was overrun by the Goths and Vandals, its influence was lost, and in any case the whole of Europe, for about 500 years, was fighting for its very survival. Civilized refinements such as perfuming the body were rapidly dumped in favour of getting enough food to eat. Somehow the religions survived, and as the priests had always been the doctors of the community, their medicinal plants, many of which were aromatic, were kept alive and propagated. As well as these, aromatic and perfumed plants continued to be used in religious ceremonies.

Using plants for perfume did not revive until the times became more settled in the Middle Ages, when the Crusades to the East started, and some of the customs, not to say plants as well, were collected by the Crusaders and taken back to Europe. During the European Dark Ages, however, the Arabs had continued the widespread and daily use of perfumes and aromas, and it was they who experimented with the then rather rudimentary technique of distillation. As a result they became highly skilled distillers of essential oils of flowers and leaves, and both the techniques and products were bound to have filtered through to the West.

With the Norman invasion of Britain, new plants started to trickle into the country, the first since the Romans had settled, and doubtless native aromatic and perfumed plants were exchanged and found their way to Continental Europe. The Normans were using *Dianthus caryophyllus* for its clove scent, to perfume wine, and the use of *Rosa gallica officinalis* is likely to have been revived by them in Britain, having originally been introduced by the Romans. All over Europe, as life calmed down and became peaceful, so the art of perfumery and the use of aromatic oils increased and became essential to daily life, in the way that they had been in classical times. 'Hungary Water' and 'Honey Water' made their appearance as eaux de toilette for use by fashionable ladies, and strewing herbs were used more and more on floors.

THE SIXTEENTH CENTURY

Scented rushes (*Acorus calamus*) were popular for strewing and later, by the time of the Elizabethans in Britain, herbs were used on floors, such as chamomile, thyme, lemon balm and costmary. The mixture of aromas produced when these leaves were walked on must have been very pleasantly pungent. Fragrant plants like lavender and rosemary were hung on walls in the houses, too.

Gradually aromas and scents came to be used in all sorts of ways: pomanders were carried in the hand or attached to belts or sashes, and necklaces were worn of pieces of aromatic gums which had set hard and had been threaded on to twine. Scented pastes were made containing rose-water, cloves, ambergris and lemon, and put into small closed dishes with holes in them, so that the perfume could diffuse out into the air.

Flower waters were sprinkled on clothes, and perfumes burnt in rooms, which were first refreshed by the burning of aromatic wood like juniper, and then scented by adding rose-water to the embers, together with sugar. This idea was carried further still by burning aromatic woods on the domestic fire; even today apple wood is used on open fires to give off its delightful scent.

Aromatics had household uses to keep away moths, fleas and other nasties, and the addition of lavender, lemon-scented leaves or powdered orris root (violet scent) would have provided sweetness to the aroma as well. Clothes not in use and hanging in 'garde-robes' or stored in chests would absorb the aroma of their containers, which were likely to be made of sandalwood or cedar, both good moth repellants.

Even clothing which was being worn came to be impregnated as a matter of course with some kind of sweet odour. Elizabeth I of England was given a pair of gloves by the Earl of Oxford, which came from Italy and were perfumed with frangipani, made from the flowers of *Plumeria rubra*. Perfumed gloves would not only smell delicious themselves but would scent the hands inside them too, and such a perfume could be made more permanent on the hands if the gloves were treated with a scented grease. Jackets, shoes, cloaks and other garments were treated; there was scented tobacco and snuff, fragrant writing paper, confectionery, soap and cosmetics, polish and cordials—the list was endless. Food was perfumed as well; for example, violet, lavender and rose conserve and primrose pottage were some popular recipes. Altogether, perfume must have completely overcome the unpleasant smells of unwashed clothing and bodies, poor sanitation, bad teeth and illness.

To produce all these scented and aromatic accessories and foods, it was necessary for most households to have a still-room, where the mixtures of oils, flower-waters, and ointments were brewed partly from the garden herbs and flowers, partly from bought substances which formed the basis of many scented recipes; amongst these were ambergris, civet and musk, storax and oil of ben, citrus peel and cloves. Orris root was popular, as were also mint, rosemary and lavender. Snuff was easily made, from powdered dried chamomile leaves, pellitory (*Parietaria judaiaca*), woodruff, peppermint and alehoof (alecost or costmary)—the flowers of pellitory bring on sneezing in no uncertain fashion.

THE SEVENTEENTH–NINETEENTH CENTURIES

So the use of perfumes and aromas accelerated and spread from mediaeval days all over Europe, through the sixteenth and seventeenth centuries, but in Britain, after Charles I was executed and the Puritans ran the country, perfume was regarded as ungodly, and its use discouraged. Moreover, there was a tax on soap, perfumed or not, and there is a suggestion that the subsequent lack of cleanliness could have contributed to the spread of the Plague in 1665. When Charles II became king, being half French, he brought with him Continental customs which included the use of perfume and aromatic herbs, and his reign saw their greatest use in Britain, which has not been exceeded since.

But the appreciation of flower perfumes gradually disappeared, coinciding with the discovery of plants from the Americas and the Far East, many of which were not scented. The style of gardening changed, too. Plants were much less featured in the large landscapes and park-size gardens which became popular during the eighteenth century than they were in the small, intimate cottage garden or the knot garden of the sixteenth century. Those plants that were grown were large, vigorous, and often flowered late in the growing season, bursting out into brilliant autumnal colours. Similarly the exotic tender plants from the Far East were dazzling in their colour display but, as noted in Chapter One, bright colour is not associated with perfume.

Perfume was not entirely lost from flowers, however, because the florist's flowers—auriculas, border carnations and pinks—became the rage in the north of Britain, being grown and hybridized by the weavers; wallflowers, violets and jonquils also continued to be grown, along with lilac and mock orange, in many of the small gardens still existing. Stocks made their appearance as bedding plants; they are of course heavily scented. Peonies and honeysuckle were still obvious, but so often goldenrod, daylilies, gaillardia, rudbeckia, the Himalayan honeysuckle (*Leycesteria formosa*), the fishbone cotoneaster and masses of rhododendrons filled the Victorian gardens, as much as anything because they were new discoveries.

Fig. 2 *A simple seventeenth-century herb garden, which was both formal and symmetrical in design, providing definition for the aromatic plants within them.*

COMMERCIAL PRODUCTION

One reason for the disappearance of fragrant and aromatic plants from the gardens was that products began to be produced commercially, so there was no longer the need for a still-room in which to store fragrant flowers and leaves. Potpourri continued to be popular, as did aromatic and fragrant sachets for clothes, and tussie-mussies, which date from the fifteenth century as 'tumose of flowrys'; all of these could easily be made at home, without the need for much expertise or knowledge.

Lavender was the first perfume produced on a large scale, at Mitcham in Surrey, in Norfolk, and at Market Deeping, and it is still harvested in Norfolk in commercial quantities. Other perfumes were 'manufactured' all over Europe through the nineteenth and into the twentieth century, but now this manufacture is mostly concentrated at Grasse, in southern France. The traditional reason for this town being the centre is that, during the Middle Ages it was one of the most important leather-curing regions; the smell of the curing leather was abominable, especially when badly done. The inhabitants looked for a way of overcoming this problem and took to perfuming the leather gloves made there. There were some famous perfumed plants growing naturally on the hills and plains behind Grasse—lavender itself, marjoram, thyme, rosemary, roses, etc.—and today mimosa, violets and jasmine are also used, but deliberately cultivated.

MODERN USE OF PERFUME

Although the liking for perfume has continued from Victorian days to the present, growing scented plants in the garden is still not as popular as it once was. However, the immense popularity of herbs and their aromas, the trend towards burning scented candles and incense in the home, the growing irritation with modern roses for not being perfumed (although this is not strictly true) and the desire to grow cottage garden plants, all seem likely to lead to the renewed planting of those 'odoriferous' species described by Thomas Hill in the first gardening book ever written in English in 1577. His list of plants to grow for a 'Garden of Pleasure and Delight' includes Stock-July-flowers, Wall-July-flowers, violets, lavender, white lilies, saffron, sweet Cicely and cowslips. We could do no better ourselves than follow his advice in the twentieth century.

Chapter Three

Cottage Garden Flowers in Spring

If one were to wander down the path of a true cottage garden in spring, especially late spring, it would be alive with colour and insects, movement, bird song and, above all, fragrance. It would be a mixture of flowering plants in all the colours of the rainbow, planted somewhat haphazardly, wherever they fitted in, and probably including such fruits as strawberries and raspberries, and the odd apple tree, old, twisted and long since in need of pruning.

Cottage gardens had their beginnings in the subsistence plot of the mediaeval peasant in which root vegetables, 'worts', and mundane greens like cabbages and leeks were grown. As time went on, a different collection of plants was gradually added to this: the herbs, mainly those supplying medicinal remedies. The variety of these must have increased greatly in Britain after the dissolution of the monasteries by Henry VIII, because the monks owned the physic gardens and were the main sources of medical help. Without these gardens, people would have resorted to 'doctoring' themselves.

At the same time, with more settled conditions throughout not only Britain, but the rest of Europe, and with the discoveries of the New World and Africa, together with the new plants which had earlier been spread through Europe by the Crusaders, there was more interest in food flavourings, and so culinary herbs were added to the mixture.

Sweet Cicely, thyme, tansy and marjoram were some of them, as well as the medicinal remedies such as rue and hyssop, feverfew and dill. The household herbs would have been especially sought after—southernwood, cotton lavender, catnep and lavender—for strewing, keeping moths and fleas at bay and scenting clothes and linen. The strong aromas of these herbs are in some cases apparent when the plants are subjected to heat, but others need to be rubbed or crushed; lavender is one of the few which has fragrance rather than aroma, and it was perhaps this shrubby ornamental herb which helped to encourage the planting of decorative varieties, again because there was no longer the pressing necessity purely to survive.

Initially, the flowering plants grown would have been the prettier of the native plants, such as foxgloves, poppies and scabious in Britain, or borage and everlasting pea in southern Europe, but gradually exotic, non-native species would have crept in to the garden, and the idea of growing plants with scented flowers would have taken hold—after all, why not grow your own perfume? Pleasant smells were very necessary in a period lacking in refrigerators and adequate sanitation, where diseases were distressingly rampant, and hygiene even for the wealthy hardly existed.

SPRING FLOWERING PLANTS

Iris

The violet fragrance is one of the main bases for manufactured perfumes, and it is found in other plants such as the flowers of *Iris reticulata* and the roots of *Iris* 'Florentina'. The little reticulate iris, only 15 cm (6 in) or so tall, flowers in early to late winter, depending on when it is planted, and has a quite definite fragrance, which does, however, need to be sniffed. It is a bulbous iris, needing good drainage, and is planted in late summer or early autumn, at a depth twice that of the length of the bulb. There are purple, blue-violet and white varieties, all good; 'Cantab' is one of the best blues.

The other iris, *I.* 'Florentina', is worth growing also for its fragrance, in spite of the fact that it is its roots which are scented. The flowers themselves have quite an astonishing aroma of chocolate. It is one of the large 'bearded' types of iris, with white flowers and purple markings. The root develops its violet fragrance as

For winter-flowering fragrance, the little Iris reticulata *is a charming example, blooming in early to mid winter.*

it dries, and becomes stronger the longer it is kept.

The Florentine iris is a native of southern Europe and was once much grown near Florence, the flower being part of the coat of arms of that city; the powdered roots are used in making frangipani, and have their best perfume when they are two or more years old.

Iris pallida is another scented iris, but with a flowery perfume, and this has been used in breeding modern scented hybrids, together with *I. germanica* and *I.* 'Florentina', which have a variety of perfumes redolent of orange blossom, vanilla, chocolate and lily-of-the-valley. Some good hybrids are 'Black Forest', purple-black flowers; 'Blue Shimmer', white flowered with blue featherings; 'Rose Violet', rose-pink 'standards' and violet 'falls', strongly and sweetly scented, and 'White City', pure white, about 1.2 m (4 ft) tall, also powerfully fragrant.

All these irises have thick fleshy rhizomes like tubers, and should be planted virtually on the surface of the soil, so that half the rhizome is exposed. They are said to like a sunny place and well-drained soil, but my own Florentine iris is in heavy soil which is waterlooged in winter, and it has not only survived but enlarged, in spite of severely cold winters. It only has sun for half the day, and flowers well, so trust your own, rather than other people's experience!

Fritillarias

Another plant which cottage gardeners took to their hearts was grown in gardens during the sixteenth century. This is the crown imperial, *Fritillaria imperialis*, described by Gerard as having been brought from Constantinople (now Istanbul); it was then a 'rare and strange Plant'. He also describes it as smelling 'very like a fox'—it certainly has an aroma rather than a fragrance, but it is such a beautiful flowering plant, it can be allowed a place, if only to contrast the sweeter smells of the other flowers.

The large 10-cm (4-in) bulb needs deep planting, spaced 20 cm (8 in) apart in deep moist soil, with some shade. The crown of orange or deep yellow flowers appears in mid spring, followed by large, green four-winged seed capsules, about 6.5 cm (2½ in) long, on the end of 90-cm (3-ft) tall stems. Plant in autumn, and work in a slug deterrent early in spring or even late winter, as slugs eat the developing shoots below the surface, and the top growth may never appear.

Wallflowers

Perhaps nothing is more associated with a cottage garden than the wallflower fragrance. Although it is not a British native, it is found wild in central Europe, and its fragrance must have assured it a place in European gardens originally. As a flowering plant, its flowers are not outstandingly beautiful, but the velvety petals in their deep, jewel-like colours of mahogany brown, red-brown, wine-purple, and occasionally orange and yellow, are worth a close look to appreciate their texture, and of course their fragrance.

Cheiranthus cheiri is well named in English, as it is quite likely to seed into a wall, and survive there regardless of cold. In the wild it is perennial, in cool climates it generally needs to be grown from seed every year, but sometimes lives through the winter and becomes perennial. Modern mixtures include Persian

Opposite:
Cheiranthus *'Harpur Crewe' is a short-lived perennial, good for growing in rock gardens.*

Carpet, mostly pastel colours, Harlequin with deep colours as well, on smallish plants, and Tom Thumb Mixed, only 15 cm (6 in) tall. Single colours are available under named varieties.

The bushiest wallflowers are obtained by pinching out the top of the main growing stems, and the biggest plants will be those sown where they are to grow and thinned to a suitable spacing, between 15 and 30 cm (6 and 12 in). Otherwise they can be sown in a nursery bed in late spring, thinned, and transplanted in early autumn. It goes without saying that they like well-drained soil, and their fragrance will be more intense in a sunny place.

The wallflower was once commonly known in Elizabethan days as the yellow stock-gilly flower, as its perfume was thought to be like that of the gilly flower or stock. It was so much used in nosegays that its botanic name relates to these—the Greek *cheir* means hand, and *anthos* is a flower. Wallflowers were also called by the name Chevisaunce—the story of this is rather a nice, though sad one. In the Middle Ages the daughter of a Scottish earl, being already forcibly engaged to the son of Robert III, fell in love with an unsuitable young man. She was imprisoned in the castle of Neidpath, and dropped a wallflower stem down to her lover to indicate her readiness to elope with him down a rope ladder; but the ladder became loose, and she was killed. The young man had only his wallflower to remind him of her, his 'chevisaunce' or 'provision for comfort'.

Centaurea

Another old cottage garden flower, introduced at the end of the sixteenth century, is often taken for granted in many gardens because of its complete reliability whatever the weather. *Centaurea montana* is a European native whose vivid blue cornflowers open in late spring. Their light purple centre has a definite aroma, of fruit and honey, but only just scenting the air round the flowers. The soft leaves are white-haired beneath, and there are also white- and lilac-flowered varieties.

If cut right down as soon as flowering finishes, it will send up a second batch of flowering stems for mid summer, and often a third display in early autumn, but it must be cut down each time. Any soil and sun or shade suit it, and it will self-seed, but without becoming a nuisance.

Aquilegia

Unexpectedly, another darling of the cottage garden is scented, unexpected because our modern hybrid versions of it are not. *Aquilegia fragrans* is a beautifully scented species from the Himalayas, with white or purple 'granny's bonnets' in late spring. The commonly grown species, *A. vulgaris*, or columbine, is a native of Europe, with an extreme tendency to promiscuity, so that seedlings will constantly appear with double, single, purple, blue, crimson, purple-blue, pink, and white flowers. The white hybrids are likely to be gently scented, too, like *A. fragrans*, but not the other colours.

While columbine will grow year after year, in sun or shade, without difficulty, *A. fragrans* needs a warm sheltered corner, with good soil drainage; its height is about 45 cm (1½ ft). An added attraction with all the aquilegias is the decorative foilage, which is prettily shaped and covers the soil well.

Peonies and primulas

Peonies and the primula family always seem to be mixed in with columbines and cornflowers in the cottage garden. The peonies flower at the same time, in late spring, the primroses, polyanthus and auriculas in early–mid spring. The primroses and polyanthus have a delicate flowery fragrance, to be appreciated by smelling the flower, rather than the air round it—the perfume is not strong enough to saturate the atmosphere. The hybrids of *Paeonia lactiflora* are much more strongly scented, such as 'Alexander Fleming', rose-pink; 'Baroness Schroeder', white flushed pale pink; 'Duchesse de Nemours', creamy white; 'Marie Crousse', salmon-pink, and 'Sarah Bernhardt', the pink of apple-blossom on white.

Auriculas, too, have an unexpectedly strong, sweet smell; somehow such perfectly formed flowers seem unlikely to be perfumed, perhaps because their perfection looks artificial. It is the border auriculas which are grown outdoors; 'Broadwell Gold' is a particularly good one, being strongly scented, deep golden and a vigorous plant with white farina on the leaves. 'Blue Velvet' is another lovely creamy white-centred purple-blue hybrid; 'Old Red Dusty Miller' has deep red-brown flowers and the leaves are floury with meal, and 'Old Suffolk Bronze' is old gold, buff and bronze in flower, with a fantastically powerful scent, much better smelt from a distance than directly from the flower.

To grow auriculas well, you need to be free of slugs and snails; given that, the next requirement is a deep moist soil and sun with a little shade some time during the day. Mulching with leafmould in early spring will cover up the crowns and keep them cool and damp.

Like their cousins the auriculas, primroses need damp cool soils and prefer some shade, even flowering where the sun never penetrates; the hybrid polyanthus do better in sun, and cowslips (*Primula veris*) also need some sun. Cowslips are native to Europe and grow wild on grassy, chalky hillsides. Although all these primula species are often grown as edging to paths or in borders with other perennials, they could well be grown scattered about in rough grass kept shortish but not lawn-like, or in the lee of shrubs or trees whose branches come down, almost but not quite, to ground level.

Bulbs and corms

Such bulbs as hyacinths and the jonquil narcissi cannot be left out of a scented cottage garden. Both the Dutch hybrid hyacinths and the earlier and looser-flowering Roman varieties are fragrant, the former so strongly that the entire garden can be scented as the spring sunshine pours down on them. Those with blue and purple flowers will have the strongest perfume.

Jonquils (*Narcissus jonquilla*) also have an almost overpowering scent; so does *N. odorus rugulosus*, its double-flowered form, *N. o.* 'Campernellii Plenus', and *N. rupicola*, a miniature daffodil from Spain. This and *N. minor*, which flowers in late winter and early spring, are good for the edge of a flowerbed, or a rock garden, anywhere there is good soil drainage. In their natural habitat, in Spain, Portugal and other Mediterranean countries, they grow in grassy slopes—the British native daffodil (not scented) grows in grass beside streams.

Cyclamen are usually regarded as being scentless, but some of the smaller pot plant strains now contain perfume as a result of deliberately using scented parents while hybridizing, and there is an outdoor species, *C. repandum*, flowering mid–late spring, which has a sweet perfume to its deep rose-red flowers. It needs shelter, and specially shade from hot summer sun, as it grows in light woodland in Greece, Crete and Rhodes; it has beautiful silver marking on the dark green leaves. With good drainage, it should grow in cool climates, provided the foliage is protected in frosty weather.

Viola and lily-of-the-valley

So gradually, scented wild plants began to be planted, and one of the first would have been violets, not the dog violet (*Viola canina*) which is unscented, but *V. odorata*, which grows much more in the open, at the foot of hedges and at the edges of fields and beside tracks and paths. Normal flowering time for violets is spring, when their delicious perfume fills the air and mingles with that of another native plant—lily-of-the-valley; both are described on pp. 115–117.

EARLY SUMMER FLOWERING PLANTS

Dividing plants arbitrarily into seasons of flowering is never strictly accurate, nor indeed satisfactory from the writing viewpoint, but it does give some idea of what plants you can associate together in the garden to give a display at any given time. The difficulty is that each season will overlap the next, and in some years the temperature may be much higher or much lower than usual at a particular time, thus retarding or forcing flowering. This of course has the bonus of resulting in some unexpected colour combinations and perfume mixes, but does make it difficult to generalize. Furthermore, some plants flower happily from spring to autumn, and cannot be categorized except under the vague term, 'summer flowering', which can mean from late spring to mid autumn, or may simply refer to a particular month.

That being the case, it is possible to have a glorious jumble of fragrant flowers in the cottage garden, varying from year to year and providing a succession of perfumes and aromas, by night as well as by day. If we walk out of our cottage front door on a summer evening, the air should be awash with odours and aromas—the sweet one of honeysuckle, the heavier one of summer jasmine, the clove-like scent of carnations and that of its near relation, sweet rocket.

Sweet rocket

Hesperis matronalis is a European wild plant, possibly also native of southern Britain though it is more likely to have been introduced; the Channel Islands are the nearest of its known habitats. It can grow 60–90 cm (2–3 ft) high, with a cluster of flowering stems—new ones appear at intervals through the summer. The longlasting flowers are pale lilac or white, rather like small wallflowers, and are strongly fragrant at night, so must be pollinated by night-flying insects. The double form is much more attractive, and similarly fragrant. Like wallflowers, sweet rocket grows best in a stony or well drained soil, even out of cracks in walls and between paving, where the single form will seed from year to year. There was once a striped double form; that has long since been lost, but since it existed once, it may turn up again as a chance mutant from a single flowered plant, when it will have to be increased from cuttings.

Bulbs

The main bulb display finishes at the end of spring, but there are still some fra-

Opposite:
Primula veris *is the cowslip whose flowers emit a delicate fragrance, elusively sweet in the air.*

grant delights in this group to come, the best ones being amongst the lilies in mid and late summer. For early summer, however, the South African summer hyacinth (*Galtonia candicans*) fills the gap; its fragrant white bells open on stems about 1.2 m (4 ft) tall, so it is a large plant, and needs space accordingly. The 10-cm (4-in) diameter bulb should go into sandy soil, planted about 20 cm (8 in) deep, in spring, and will do best in a sunny place. This is another bulb like *F. imperialis* which needs slug bait planted with it.

Pinks and carnations

One of the most scented and popular groups of cottage garden flowers has been grown in cultivation for centuries, reaching back to the classical times of the Romans and Greeks, if not earlier. The pinks and carnations are delightful flowering plants well worth growing for their appearance alone. Their foliage of narrow pointed leaves is evergreen, or rather evergrey, a silvery grey or grey-green, depending on the variety, which makes neat hummocks all year round, and when in flower during early and mid summer, they produce a mass of rounded single or double flowers in a truly kaleidoscopic range of reds, pinks, crimson, magenta, purple, salmon and white. Their perfume is their chief asset, the quality for which they are renowned, a strong clove-like, spicy scent which fills the air round them and makes them essential plants for the fragrant garden.

Various writers have written extensively about these flowers. Their history is long; they have been widely grown and used for culinary and household uses, and they hybridize easily so that many varieties have been produced. Gerard said: '. . . a great and large volume would not suffice to write of every one at large in particular', because every year new varieties were produced from different countries and climates. He was given a yellow one from Poland (this in 1597), and even in those Elizabethan days they had a plethora of common names, some of which were: clove gillofloure, pagiants and sops-in-wine. Gilliflower is still listed in the modern Royal Horticultural Society's Dictionary of Gardening, sometimes spelt gillyflower, derived from the French *giroflée*, Italian *garofolo*, Greek *karyophillon*, and finally Arabic *quaranful*, a clove. Sops-in-wine is a reference to the fact that the Spanish in the days of the Romans added the flowers to wine to spice up the flavour; the word carnation meant in Gerard's day 'flesh colour', or it could have been derived from the use of the flowers in chaplets (crowns).

The wild carnation, *Dianthus caryophyllus*, is a native of southern Europe, which may have arrived in Britain along with the building stone brought by the Normans for their castles and churches. Its flowers are single, rose-pink, and appear mid–late summer; from it have come, by hybridization with other dianthus species, a vast tribe of beautifully flowered plants whose double flowers include orange and yellow as well amongst their colouring—the only one missing is blue. Types of flowers are: Picotée, Flakes (marbled petals) and Bizarres—all striped—and collecting the different kinds is a fascinating occupation.

Not all are scented, however, as a result of breeding, and care has to be taken if you regard fragrance as essential. Any variety with the word 'clove' in the name is certain to be acceptable, such as 'Oakfield Clove', deep crimson, and 'Snow Clove', pure white. There used to be a 'Yellow Clove', the first of this colour to

Opposite:
The white or purple shades of dianthus will always have a pungent clove perfume; other colours are often not scented.

be scented, but it is no longer listed. However, it may still be growing somewhere, waiting to be rediscovered.

The carnations must have a fully sunny position; they don't like lingering damp in any form, so good drainage is also essential, and alkalinity is important. Cold is no problem, and they are perennial, growing 45–60 cm (18–24 in) tall. They need a spacing of 30 cm (12 in) between each plant.

The wild pinks are *D. plumarius*, and in spite of their name can be white, as well as pink, with feathery petals. They flower from early to late summer, and naturally are most likely to be found growing out of walls. Height is between 10 and 30 cm (4 and 12 in), but the rather weak stems make them appear quite low-growing. As with the carnations, many hybrids have been produced from this, crossed with *D. caryophyllus* and other dianthus species; the flowers are smaller and more likely to be single, though there are double-flowered forms. Interestingly, the name of the flower has been given to the colour and not the other way round; the colour was not named as such with any frequency until the late 1700s, and the word is perhaps derived from the Dutch name for the flower, *pink-oog*, meaning a small winking eye.

Pinks had the same common names as carnations, and they were in every cottage garden, though there were fewer varieties, until the Laced pinks arrived in the nineteenth century, hybridized by the Paisley weavers in Scotland, and characterized by a dark border the same colour as the centre, and by rounded, not fringed petals.

The most famous pink is probably 'Mrs Sinkins', a white fimbriated double,

Fig. 3 Dianthus *'Mrs Sinkins'*

about 30 cm (12 in) tall, with a powerful fragrance indeed, bred by the Master of Slough workhouse in the 1870s and named for his wife. It is still a strong and vigorous plant. Not far behind it in reputation is 'Dad's Favourite', basically white, but with a lacing of deep red, and a purple centre. 'Fenbow's Nutmeg Clove' has small, maroon-crimson, double flowers and a powerful aroma of nutmeg; it may date from Chaucer's time, the fourteenth century.

Others are: 'Sam Barlow', a white double, rather an untidy flower, but with a maroon blotch at the base of its petals and a penetrating aroma; 'Queen of Sheba', a laced pink from Elizabethan days, magenta purple on a white ground with serrated petals; 'Caesar's Mantle', very dark red, toothed and strongly scented; 'Fountains Abbey', black edging on white, fringed; 'Bridal Veil', double white fringed, with red centre; 'Little Old Lady' ('Chelsea Pink'), small, double, deep red, with splashes of white, particularly strong perfume.

Pinks need even better drainage than carnations, and are liable to grow in nothing but sand and chalk with no apparent discomfort. They are less bushy than carnations, more inclined to straggle and lie along the ground, but have a superb fragrance, flowering intermittently from early to late summer. Planting should be at 23 cm (9 in) intervals in autumn or spring—preferably plant in spring in areas where winters are inclined to be wet.

CHAPTER FOUR

HIGH SUMMER IN THE COTTAGE GARDEN

There are one or two plants which flower in mid and late summer whose genus is not normally regarded as a scented one. However, they are exceptions worth growing; for instance the yellow daylily, *Hemerocallis lutea*, has a distinct and sweet perfume coming from its lemon yellow trumpets. It is a neat daylily which does not get out of hand and spread all over a border; the flowers are in proportion, and it flowers for about three weeks.

BULBS AND CORMS

Lilies

One of the most exotic and strongest perfumes comes from lilies, and close to, it is very strong—it smells unpleasant and is much better absorbed from the air at some distance from the plants. Not all lilies are perfumed by any means, but of those that are, one of the favourites which has been grown in cottage gardens in Europe since the time of the Romans is *Lilium candidum*, the Madonna lily. The scented lilies are practically all white, yellow or purple, and this one is no exception, having 12–20 white, bell-shaped flowers in a cluster at the top of 1.2-m (4-ft) stems in early to mid-summer. Its flowers are clearly recognizable on Cretan vases of 1750 BC, and it is known to have been cultivated since 300 BC, mainly in the Middle East. From this lily have come the scented Cascade hybrids, bred by the American lily specialist Jan de Graaff.

Planting should be late summer to early autumn, with about 5 cm (2 in) of soil above it, preferably an alkaline one; the variety *L.c. salonikae* is just the same, but disease-resistant, and will set fertile seed.

Lilium auratum, the golden-rayed lily of Japan, is a magnificent lily, the queen of the garden, growing at least 1.5 m (5 ft) tall, with a cluster of large, white trumpet flowers about 23 cm (9 in) wide, with a band of golden-yellow from inside the lower part of the throat to the tip, and with wine-purple spots in the throat. There should be six of these flowers if the bulb is grown in any average soil, but with good soil and feeding, there can be 20 or more, and height will be 2.1 m (7 ft). This is one with an overpowering scent, filling the air for yards round it, and lasting up to eight weeks during late summer and autumn. From this plant many lovely hybrids have been produced, although for me I have to say that the original cannot be improved upon.

Lilium regale, *the regal lily, is well named both for its beautiful white and gold trumpet flowers, and its strong, sweet perfume.*

A sunny position is necessary, sheltered from wind, and an acid soil is essential—nothing less will do and neutral is no substitute. Good drainage is also important, so sand or grit should be mixed with the soil beforehand and at planting time. The bulb needs to be planted deep, between 15 and 30 cm (6 and 12 in), in spring, and should have some good, fleshy roots on it. If not, plant it in a container for the first season, so that it can develop them with some protection.

The regal lily, *L. regale*, is not difficult to grow and is a fairly recent discovery (1901) from China; it has large white trumpets with a golden throat and deep pink flushing on the outside of the trumpet, which is strongly and sweetly perfumed. Height is about 1.5 m (5 ft) and flowering time is mid summer. It needs sun and a soil free from waterlogging, acid to slightly alkaline in reaction, and the bulb should be planted about 20 cm (8 in) deep in mid autumn. As with all these lilies, use a slug deterrent if there is the slightest suspicion that they might be a problem.

There are many more scented lilies, and unfortunately space does not permit detailed descriptions, but a selection is as follows: *L. amabile*, red flowers; *L. cernuum*, mauve; *L. henryi*, orange-yellow; *L. longiflorum*, white; *L. martagon*, purple, fragrant at night; *L. speciosum*, white and red spotted; *L. testaceum*, yellow-orange.

Gladioli

The large-flowered gladioli hybrids have the most beautiful flowers, exquisitely coloured; they are of such perfection as to be unreal and, like rhododendrons, need to be viewed in small quantities. But the lily is not gilded—they have no perfume, and for that it is necessary to grow some species, for instance *G. tristis*, one of the oldest varieties in cultivation. It was introduced from Natal and grown at the Chelsea Physic Garden, London, in 1745. The yellow flowers, spotted with red, grow in a one-sided spike on stems about 45 cm (18 in) tall, and are scented in the evening and at night. *G. liliaceus* is also fragrant at night, its large brown-yellow flowers pollinated by nocturnal moths. There are other scented gladioli, for instance *G. carinatus*, violet coloured and violet-scented; *G. hirsutus*, pink-flowered and clove-scented and *G. recurvus*, yellow and shades of blue, violet-scented. All are South African, but they are not available in Britain.

Gladioli need very good soil drainage, and plenty of sun; the corms are planted in early to late spring, and the stems supported with canes as soon as the buds can be seen. In cool–temperate climates they should be dug up and over-wintered in a frostproof place. As a garden flower, they are probably at their best in a sunny border mixed with other plants, and used alongside a path; a row of gladioli would be too formal for a cottage garden.

Crinums

Crinum × powellii is an exceedingly handsome plant with large, deep pink, lily-like flowers in clusters at the top of fleshy stems in early-mid autumn. It is of South African origin and is a large plant for a bulb, with leaves at least 90 cm (3 ft) long and a flower stem 60 cm (2 ft) tall; the bulbs have a diameter of 15 cm (6 in) and need to be planted in late spring with the same depth of soil above them, i.e. they need a hole 30 cm (12 in) deep.

These crinums get their perfume from the parent *C. bulbispermum*, which was introduced to cultivation about 250 years ago. Most of their hardiness comes from it, too; even so, they need shelter and a warm, south facing border at the foot of a wall, so that they can thrive in cool–temperate climates. It is a good idea to mulch them heavily in autumn for frost protection.

ANNUALS AND BIENNIALS

Some annuals grown for bedding in summer are unexpectedly scented, too; iberis, petunia and nemesia are three of them normally grown purely for their colouring.

Iberis
The iberis is the white-flowered annual species of candytuft, *I. amara*, said by some authorities to be a British native, by others to be a garden escape. There is no doubt, however, that it grows naturally in the warmer parts of Europe, and has been hybridized from the original 15-cm (6-in) species into giants 38 cm (15 in) tall, some coloured in shades of pink, lilac, purple and red, and less strongly scented. *I. odorata* is also scented, but not available in Britain, which is a pity, as it is more strongly scented; its flowers are white, appearing in late summer.

Petunia
Petunias have changed to a vast degree since the original *P. integrifolia* and *P. nyctaginiflora* were introduced early in the last century from South America. Along with them came another, variously called *P. violacea, Nierembergia gracilis* and *N. phoenicea*. Whatever it is, it comes from South America, where it grows as a perennial with purplish, tubular flowers in mid–late summer. Although not now available in Britain, it would be worth tracking down perhaps from Argentina itself. It would make the bedding petunias currently grown into perfect flowers if it were used in breeding to introduce scent.

Nemesia
Nemesias are charming small bedding plants, grown from seed started in warmth early in the year. They, too, have come a long way from *N. strumosa*, with its great variability in the colour range red, yellow and orange; modern selections have blue-flowered varieties as well. None has scent, though, and to introduce this *N. floribunda* would have to be used, similarly native to South Africa, with white and yellow flowers. Again this species is not available, but it is worth trying to find for growing in cool–temperate climates, and mixing it with a planting of nemesias such as Carnival Mixed, Blue Gem or Mello Red and White.

Tobacco plants
The tobacco plant is renowned for its heavy perfume, especially in the evening, and is another half-hardy annual in cool–temperate climates, but if the winters are mild it can survive to be a short-lived perennial. Height varies between 30 and 90 cm (12 and 36 in), depending on the strain, though about 38 cm (15 in) is the average, and colours are white, pink, rose, wine, red, crimson and green. Be warned, though: not all today's hybrids are scented—the one called 'Lime Green' is not. If you get the mixture called Evening Fragrance, you will be certain of perfume, and a good range of colours, on plants 90 cm (3 ft) tall. There is also a selection whose flowers are bunched together, facing upwards on shorter stems, but I prefer the taller, more graceful ones.

Nicotiana tabacum is the plant whose leaves are used for tobacco, a native of South America, growing 1.2 m (4 ft) tall, and with rose coloured flowers. It was described in detail by Gerard in 1597: 'the dry leaves are used to be taken in a pipe set on fire and suckt into the stomacke, and thrust forth againe at the nostrils, against the paines in the head, rheumes and aches in any part of the bodie'.

For perfume at night, grow Matthiola bicornis, *the night-scented stock, with single flowers in a variety of delicate shades of purple and pink.*

Opposite: *Tobacco plants are a species which are moth-pollinated and at their most fragrant in the evening.*

Stocks

Many of the fragrant flowers are pollinated by night-flying insects, and have their strongest perfume in the evening and through the night; tobacco plants are one, and the night-scented stock is another. *Matthiola bicornis*, another member of the *Cruciferae* family like wallflowers, sweet rocket and candytuft, is a rather straggling annual to 30 cm (12 in) tall whose flowers are pale purple, or lilac to white in summer. Its perfume is out of all proportion to its appearance and, once established in the garden, it will self-seed into cracks in paving and at the foot of house walls.

Matthiola incana is the species from which the garden stocks have descended, i.e. the Brompton, 10-week, autumn-flowering (East Lothian) and winter-flowering kinds. Strictly speaking only the 10-week and autumn-flowering ones should be described here but discussing them altogether prevents much turning of pages and wasting time. The height of the Bromptons is about 45 cm (18 in), in a colour range of pink, rose, crimson, white and lavender, and seed should be sown in mid–late summer for flowering in late spring the following year. Plant them where they are to flower in mid autumn or overwinter them under frames or cloches and plant out in early spring.

Ten-week stocks flower within that number of weeks from sowing the seed in early to mid spring with a little heat of 18°C (65°F). Height is 23–60 cm (9–24 in), and colours include all those given above, plus apricot and pale yellow. The East Lothian stocks are similar, and flower in early autumn, though sown at the same time as the 10-week stocks.

For winter-flowering, seed is sown in mid summer, and the plants grown on in pots, potting on as required, but flowering them under cover, not outdoors, in a conservatory or greenhouse in countries where winters are frosty. Whatever kind is grown, the dark green-leaved seedlings should be discarded, as these produce only single flowers, not double ones.

The original stock, *M. incana*, is a maritime plant, and one writer recommended in 1757 that the compost in which the seeds are sown should be watered with brine before sowing, and sea-sand should be used in making up the compost. Confusingly, they were also called gilly flowers, like the carnations, but were distinguished by being named 'stock-gilly flowers' or 'stock gillofers'. The Brompton stocks acquired their name from the nurserymen London & Wise who had their nursery in the Brompton Road, and who raised both 'purple and stript' varieties for the gardens of the new Blenheim Palace.

Heliotrope

If you want a fragrance with a difference, heliotrope is the plant; the fragrance itself is quite familiar, but is unusual to be associated with a flower. *Heliotropium peruvianum* comes from Peru and has purple or white flowers tinted with lilac, heavily perfumed with the smell of almond. Cherry pie is its country name—perhaps cooked cherries do smell of almonds? It is not hardy and has always been used for summer garden displays, originally as a 60–90 cm (2–3 ft) standard with a head of dark green leaves and violet flowers, now more often as a much lower growing bushy plant about 30 cm (12 in) tall. 'Chatsworth' is deep purple, with a strong fragrance; 'Marine', 60 cm (2 ft) and 'Mini Marine', 38 cm (15 in) are similarly coloured modern varieties.

Heliotropium *'Chatsworth'* produces an unusual and strong, sweet fragrance of almond, late in the summer when few other flowers are scented.

Verbena

There is another annual, half-hardy in cool–temperate climates, which is rather like heliotrope to look at as regards its flowers, though it is not shrubby, and that is verbena. It is related to heliotrope in that its family, the *Verbenaceae*, follows that of heliotrope, the *Boraginaceae*, in botanical development. The *Labiaceae* are similarly close and have many aromatic plants in their group, but the verbenas are not generally odorous, although the group includes lemon verbena (*Lippia citriodora*) as well as verbena.

Small but spreading, the modern hybrids are heavily floriferous in a mixture of all colours, often with a white 'eye'. Their ancestry includes the scented *V. teucrioides* whose white flowers are fragrant in the evening. Those which are shades of purple, lilac and white are the scented kinds, while red, crimson and similar shades will be odourless, as is their parent, the scarlet-flowered *V. peruviana*.

From South America, the verbenas were first introduced to cultivation in Europe and elsewhere during the early 1700s, but *V. officinalis* is a native of Europe including Britain, and was much used as a medicinal and magical herb, especially by the Druids who called it *ferfaen*, witches' herb, from which comes our modern vervain; however, it has no perfume or aroma.

Sweetpea

One of the most loved and famous of scented annuals is *Lathyrus odoratus*, the sweetpea. The strong, sweet, flowery perfume of this delicately coloured flowering climber is the essence of long hot summer days, nostalgic of childhood, recalling country gardens and seaside holidays, cats basking in the sun and tea on the lawn.

In spite of these associations, *L. odoratus* is not one of the older cottage garden plants, though the appearance and habit of its hybrids qualify it admirably for such gardens. It comes from Sicily and was first mentioned by a monk, Abbé Franciscus Cupani, in a herbal of 1697; two years later he sent seeds to a British schoolmaster who lived at Enfield and who owned some of the first hothouses built in Britain, in which he could germinate the seeds. The flowers of the original species are small, with magenta and red petals, and the plant is rather weedy, but the characteristic perfume is strong.

Perhaps a dozen varieties appeared as sports during the next 150 years, but in 1870 a Mr Henry Eckford decided to try and produce new varieties by cross-pollinating—the sweetpea is self-fertile, so practically no natural hybridizing would occur. He succeeded; 30 years later he exhibited 115 new varieties at the Bicentenary Sweetpea Exhibition at the Crystal Palace. In 1908 a variety with frilled petals appeared spontaneously, to be called 'Countess Spencer' and the following year another appeared in the garden of Mr W. J. Unwin. He also began to breed them and so the well known seed firm was begun, and continues to thrive today, still renowned for its sweetpeas.

To grow superb sweetpeas with five or more flowers on a stem, you will need a strong rich soil containing plenty of rotted organic matter. Trenching really is the best preparation for the soil, digging two spades deep, in early spring. Choose a windproof place, and use 2.4-m (8-ft) canes penetrating 30 cm (1 ft) into the soil

Opposite:
These Jetset sweetpeas follow the colour rule for perfume: the white and lavender coloured ones will have the sweetest scent.

for support, spaced 25 cm (10 in) apart. Sow the seed singly in sweetpea tubes, and pinch out the growing point just above the third pair of leaves, to give two strong shoots; remove all other sideshoots. Sowing can be done in early autumn and the plants overwintered in frames, with slug protection, or in early spring in frames, planting out in mid–late spring, again with slug protection.

Train each shoot singly up a cane, attached with split rings or ties, and remove all sideshoots and tendrils. When the plants reach the cane top they can be taken down and layered, taking them up the third, fourth or fifth cane along, to get more growth and further flowering. Those over-wintered will start to flower in early summer, the others near the end of mid summer.

Rather than grow them in rows for superb exhibition flowers, you can grow them over arches and pergolas, up house walls and round front doors, or covering wooden poles and tree stumps. Wherever grown, protect from slugs and snails, as they adore the small plants.

There are so many varieties now, and all lovely, choice is difficult, but to be sure of perfume, choose blue, purple, magenta, white or cream flowers; sometimes the red or pink ones are scented. Like most hybrids, they vary considerably from the original wild species: if the colour is greatly different the hybrid concerned is likely to be difficult to grow. Thus blue, purple, magenta and red sweetpeas should be strong with plenty of flower and fragrance, those which are salmon or pink will be smaller flowered, unscented and less vigorous.

Some varieties have a perfume which is reliably penetrating and old-fashioned: 'Charlie's Angel', blue and lavender; 'Cream Southborne', creamy frilled flowers; 'Champagne Bubbles', creamy yellow and buff; 'Charles Unwin', pink; 'Ballerina', cream with rose-pink picotee edges; 'Old Times', cream and blue; 'Evensong', blue and lilac; 'The Doctor', mauve; 'Percy Thrower', lilac; 'Cambridge Blue,' pale blue.

Alternatively there is a super-scented Old Fashioned Mixture, of various colours, with smaller but heavily scented flowers; there is an interestingly coloured named one of these called 'America' which is crimson and white striped, and there are other named old fashioned kinds in different colours to be obtained separately. The Knee-hi mixture grows to 45 cm (18 in); it does not need stopping and can be supported by twiggy brush-wood. Jetset is 90 cm (3 ft) tall with an abundance of flowers; 'Snoopea' is about 60 cm (2 ft), without tendrils and needing no support. These short mixtures fill small narrow borders nicely.

Mignonette

Mignonette is a typical cottage garden flower—hardy, scented and easily grown. *Reseda odorata* is a hardy annual grown from seed sown outdoors in a sunny, well-drained place—it makes an ideal edging to a bed or path—and grows into small sturdy plants about 23 cm (9 in) tall, with clusters of tiny yellowish flowers, not particularly attractive, but overwhelmingly perfumed.

It is a native of Egypt and North Africa and was probably introduced to Europe in 1752. A century later it had become so popular that every window-box in London contained mignonette, so that the perfume was almost druglike in its strength. We might well copy this today, to overcome the smell of exhaust fumes. The French called it mignonette or 'little darling' and the Empress Josephine grew it in pots on her balconies and terraces, from seed sent by Napoleon, so the story goes, whilst in the thick of his Egyptian campaign. *R. odorata* has the strongest perfume, but the modern forms are almost as good and have larger flower clusters, brownish tinged as well as yellow.

Evening primrose

The evening primrose (*Oenothera biennis*) is also a lovely cottage garden flower and has naturalized in European conditions. It has grown wild since its introduction from North America, probably in 1619. It opens its bright yellow, saucer-shaped flowers from early summer to mid autumn up stems 1.2–1.8 m (4–6 ft) tall, and is an evening bloomer, the fragrance attracting the nocturnal moths which help in its pollination. As it is a biennial, seed needs to be sown in late spring, the small plants transplanted, and then overwintered, but it is perfectly hardy. It needs little care in cultivation and this, together with its beauty and fragrance—and the fact that it self-seeds—must make it one of the best value-for-space plants ever grown in the garden.

Silene

There are some pretty flowers amongst the campions and catchflies, natives of Europe including Britain. The sea campion (*Silene maritima*) has a charming white frilly flower on a shortish perennial plant about 30 cm (12 in) tall, but not scented; the night-flowering annual catchfly (*S. noctiflora*) is fragrant, but only as the temperature falls. Then its pink flowers will be wide open all night, partially closing with the light to show their yellow undersides. *S. nutans* is the Nottingham catchfly, with narrow white petals reflexed back towards the stem, growing to about 45 cm (18 in) and flowering from late spring to autumn; its perfume is undisputed, reminiscent of pinks, and best at night. Cultivation of these catchflies is easy in most soils; they could be grown in rough grass as well as mixed in with other flowering plants.

PERENNIALS

Bergamot

The argument about aromas on page 78 could wellbe continued in the cottage garden, as marigolds are very much a cottage garden plant, both the calendulas or pot marigolds, and the tagetes, French and African, from New Mexico. Whatever their generic name, marigolds are strongly aromatic and rather bitterly so. Some aromas are undoubtedly pleasant, usually the fruity or spicy ones, others are not, like the marigolds, so I will pass rapidly on to another aromatic cottage plant, the bergamot (*Monarda didyma*), whose pointed dark green leaves smell strongly of the bergamot orange. This was itself an orange–lemon hybrid named after Bergamo, in northern Italy, and the oil of its fruits was popular for perfumery use in the seventeenth century.

The perennial bergamot is American, and is also called oswego tea; it grew on the shores of Lake Ontario at Oswego, where it was used for tea, and was one of John Bartram's plants. The aroma of the leaves goes well with white wine, and they can be dried and used for linen sachet mixtures or in potpourri. The species has a scarlet mophead for a flower on stems about 60 cm (2 ft) tall, and it will be in flower continuously from early summer to early autumn. Another with aromatic, citrus-scented leaves is *M. citriodora*, strongly lemony, and with pink flowers. There is a variety of hybrids of *M. didyma* available, but with less sweet-smelling leaves, for instance 'Croftway Pink', rose-pink; 'Blue Stocking', violet-purple; 'Prairie Night', light purple; and 'Mahogany', very deep crimson brown.

A medium to moist soil and an open or sunny position will encourage large clumps to grow; monarda does not do well in heavy shade or dry soil.

Fig. 4 *Monarda didyma (bergamot)*

Phlox

For foreigners trying to learn English, the word for 'gatherings of sheep' is another exasperating example of the sound being the same as that for another word, while the spelling is quite different. Phlox are a perennial garden plant introduced to cultivation about 250 years ago from America, by John Bartram, a botanist and plant collector. *P.* × *decussata* are the border perennials, the first introduced having a mauve flower and being grown in south London at a garden in Eltham. From this have come the great range of flower colours that can now be grown, mainly in the mauve, slaty blue, pink and lilac shades, some with white eyes, produced on plants that reach between 60 and 90 cm (2 and 3 ft) tall.

Phlox hybrids have a curious aroma which, like that of privet flowers, you either love or hate; certainly it is better in the evening when it can be called a fragrance, but in the daytime it is sneeze-making. Whatever it is, the scent is a strong

The burning bush, Dictamnus albus purpureus, *gives off so much essential oil on a warm day that it can be set alight.*

one, provided at a time of the year when other flowers are beginning to die off rather than starting to bloom, in late summer to autumn. The colours are lovely, and groups of phlox are quite dazzling, mixing well into the cottage garden scene. They need moist soil and a little shade—a quick-draining soil is quite unsuitable. They should be planted in late autumn unless the soil is really damp, when a spring planting will be more satisfactory.

The species *P. maculata* and *P. paniculata* are both purple-flowered and have a much more acceptable and sweeter scent; if you are choosing the hybrids for perfume look for the purple-mauve or white flowered ones, such as 'Little Lovely', purple with white eye; 'Frau Buchner', white; or 'Iver', lilac-mauve. A phlox with a difference is 'Norah Leigh', since its leaves have yellow margins, but the purple flowers are smaller than those of other hybrids.

Asphodeline and Asphodelus

Asphodeline lutea is often confused with asphodelus, in spite of the latter having mainly white flowers. Both are scented, though, with spikes of flowers in mid summer; *Asphodeline lutea* grows to about 90 cm (3 ft), *Asphodelus ramosus* to 1.5 m (5 ft) and *A. fistulosus* to barely 50 cm (20 in). Neither genus is difficult to grow, and both are ornamental as well as scented. They were once much seen in European, and then British gardens in the sixteenth century. Before that, many centuries earlier, they were widespread on the coasts of Mediterranean countries, and the roots were eaten by the Greeks as part of their normal diet; this could account for their modern reduction in the wild.

Burning Bush

Like bergamot, the burning bush (*Dictamnus albus*) is aromatic rather than fragrant. The whole plant carries an odour, and particularly the leaves, which smell pleasantly of citrus when rubbed or bruised. Height can be 75 cm (2¹/₂ ft), and its spread nearly as much, and it is topped in early to mid summer by clusters of large white flowers centred with long, spidery stamens. On a hot sunny day without wind, the essential oils become so volatile that the air above the plant is saturated with the vapour, which can be set alight.

A native of eastern Europe and Asia, dictamnus is a long-lived plant preferring well-drained soil and plenty of sun. Once planted, it should not be disturbed as the fleshy roots do not take kindly to being broken, so choose its site carefully. There is a pink-purple flowered form, *D. a. purpureus*, which is delicately attractive, to blend with other pinks, lavenders and lilacs in a long border or one of the island variety. When flowering is over, both this and the white-flowered species have ornamental winged seed-pods in autumn, worth keeping for dried flower decoration, and remaining aromatic through the winter.

SCENTED-LEAVED PELARGONIUMS

Continuing the aromatic leaf theme, there are the scented-leaved geraniums (*Pelargonium* spp), not truly hardy in cool–temperate climates, being natives of South Africa, though they grow perfectly well outdoors in warm–temperate and sub-tropical areas. However, they grew indoors on every cottage windowledge in Britain when they were first introduced, and can perfectly well be grown outdoors from late spring to early autumn, to fill gaps in borders and add additional aromas to the fragrances already being carried in the air.

These scented-leaved pelargoniums contain an astonishing collection of perfumes and aromas. When they were first introduced in the seventeenth century, in the shape of *Pelargonium triste*, they were almost more of a curiosity than anything else, because this one has dull coloured flowers in mid summer, small and brownish, sometimes with a yellow colour as well, but with an unexpected and strong sweet perfume from twilight onwards. Its carrot-like leaves are aromatic, and it has a thick tuberous root, so altogether it is not very typical of pelargoniums, but many varieties came from it and were grown outdoors by the end of the century for the fragrance of the flowers. About a century later another one with scented flowers appeared, *P. gibbosum*, which has small yellow flowers in early summer and whose fragrance becomes apparent only after dark; its stems are peculiarly swollen at the leaf joints.

The scented-leaved kinds took about two centuries, however, before they really made their mark, and then they became exceedingly popular for indoor growth in conservatories and on windowsills. The flowers are small and usually pink, lilac, pink-purple, coral, white and shades of these colours; the leaves are variously and interestingly shaped, some of them being deeply dissected, some of them soft and velvety in texture, and with this comes the striking range of perfumes and aromas. A few of them are: 'Attar of Roses', small plant, with feathery, rose-scented leaves and lavender flowers; 'Clorinda', large leaves, eucalyptus-scented; *P. crispum* 'Variegatum', tightly curled leaves with yellow edges, strongly lemon-scented; *P.* × *fragrans*, small kidney-shaped leaves, pine-scented; *P. odoratissimum*, rounded, light green velvet leaves, apple-scented; *P. tomentosum*, grey-green soft leaves, peppermint-scented; 'Prince of Orange', small, orange-scented leaves.

Most are small bushy plants, easily grown outdoors in a sunny place and with average to light well-drained soil. Pinching out the tips of shoots will make them bushier still, and provide more of the small flowers. The leaves dry well and add a good deal of aroma to potpourris, or can be used in linen sachets. Cuttings root easily, so new plants can be obtained each season without difficulty.

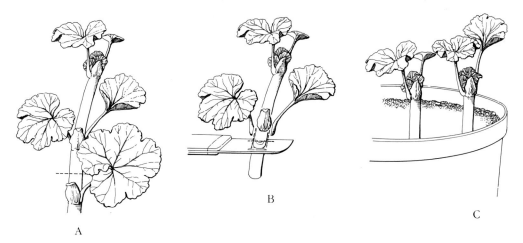

A

B

C

Fig. 5 *Increase by tip cuttings.*
    (a) *Cut the tip off a young shoot about 7.5 cm (3 in) long.*
    (b) *Trim cleanly just below a leaf joint; remove lowest leaves.*
    (c) *Put in compost up to half the length of the cutting.*

CHAPTER FIVE

FRAGRANT BOSKAGE

The woody plants are the most rewarding to grow for the sake of their fragrance, and the shrubs in particular are good for gardens. Their flowers are strong and sweetly scented; since the plants carrying them are large, they fill a correspondingly large area with perfume, and there are so many it is possible to keep a succession of fragrances and aromas going all through the year. Climbing woody plants such as honeysuckle add to the choice, and there are also trees with fragrant or aromatic foliage as well as scented flowers.

This group of plants supplies the bulk and framework of most gardens. Without shrubs and trees, a garden has no excitement in it; there is no element of surprise because the whole garden consists of beds and borders and lawn or paving. Of course you can vary the landscape with fences and walls, flights of steps and slopes and so on, but then the garden aspect appears belittled.

The rounded, three-dimensional shapes of shrubs provide the quality of softness required by a true garden which contains more plants than hardware. Furthermore, they give shelter and ensure warmth for plants, animals and humans; they provide privacy when used as hedges or screens, and they help to contain gardens within gardens, the secret places that no garden should be without, embellished with fragrance. The taller shrubs, climbing species and trees give the garden a better contrast to the monotonous, horizontal plane.

A garden without trees is inconceivable. They give so much to it: free organic matter all year and particularly in autumn; shelter from wind and hot sun; food and homes for birds, insects and other creatures, and beauty of form, foliage and flower. Yet they are usually taken for granted and fade into the ignored background. They should be given as much importance in the garden's design as flower beds or rock gardens, not relegated to a place on the boundary or used to block the prevailing wind.

SPRING-FLOWERING SHRUBS AND TREES

Choisya
One of the most powerfully fragrant shrubs is the one familiarly known as Mexican orange blossom (*Choisya ternata*), native to that country, where it can grow as much as 3 m (10 ft) tall. In cool–temperate climates it is more likely to grow to 1.5–1.65 m (5–5$^1/_2$ ft), with a rounded spreading growth habit requiring a space of

Choisya ternata is the Mexican orange blossom, well named since its white flowers closely resemble the citrus flowers, both in looks and fragrance.

at least 1.8 m (6 ft) when fully grown.

The five-petalled white flowers are clustered at the end of shoots in late spring to early summer, and smell strongly of orange blossom, a wonderful perfume which scents the air all around the bush. After a mild winter it starts to flower in early spring, and can easily have a second flowering in early autumn. The glossy light green, evergreen leaves are decorative, too, arranged in threes horizontally; there is now a variety called 'Sundance', about 90 cm (3 ft) tall, which has light yellow leaves. It is not as strong or fast-growing, but is still fragrant and provides a burst of light amongst other, darker evergreens.

The Mexican orange blossom is hardier than its namesake but not completely so; it will have to be given sun and good soil drainage, and even so, is likely to be cut back by frost, and killed if the frost is severe. Pruning is unnecessary except to tidy. The edge of a sunny patio is an ideal place for it, since its rather formal appearance combines well with the regular lines of paving; a warm wall protecting it from the north will be required in a cool garden.

Elaeagnus

The more I garden, the more I appreciate the usefulness and decorative qualities of foliage. Flowers are lovely but evanescent; leaves last the whole season, sometimes all year round, and there is extraordinary variation in their shape and colour, which does not become apparent until one has gardened for some time. The elaeagnus genus, or oleaster, for instance, has some extremely handsome foliage amongst its species, much more showy than the flowers, which are mostly tiny and unassumingly coloured.

The silver berry, *E. commutata*, is one of these, with really silvery, quite large leaves, nearly 10 cm (4 in) long, and almost as wide. The oval fruit is silvery too, but the yellowish flowers produced before them, in early summer, are only 1.5 cm ($^1/_2$ in) long, though there are a great many. Their fragrance and sphere of influence is considerable, especially as this shrub grows at least 1.8 m (6 ft) tall, sometimes up to 3.6 m (12 ft). If only it was evergreen . . .

Nearly all the elaeagnus in cultivation have fragrant flowers, other species are *E. macrophylla*, *E. angustifolia* and *E. multiflora*, but the silver berry is much the most attractive. In soil that suits it, it will sucker and become a nuisance; such a soil will be sandy, in which it will be the best colour, especially if grown in a really sunny place. It is a shrub that asks to be made much of and given a position as a specimen, sheltered from cold wind. Again, pruning is not necessary.

Laburnum

Following the Mexican orange blossom, the silver berry provides a link between that and laburnum, a small tree which has become such a standard planting in gardens that it is almost invisible. Its brilliant yellow waterfalls of blossom are not any the less decorative, and the species *L. alpinum* has the most fragrant pea flowers, in hanging clusters looking like a yellow form of wisteria, about 30 cm (12 in) long. Flowering is late for a laburnum, early or even mid summer, depending on location. *L.* × *watereri* 'Vossii' has even longer clusters, 60 cm (2 ft) when well-grown, also scented, flowering from late spring into early summer. The perfume of both is more pronounced on a warm evening.

There are no problems in growing laburnums; any soil suits them except very wet ones. They need strong staking until well established, and their lifespan can be lengthened by removal of the seedpods, of which a great many are set. As the seeds are even more poisonous than the rest of the tree, removal is a useful precaution. With the beautiful blossom of these two varieties, so much better than the common form, it is worth making one a specimen tree as an eye-catcher, on or beside a lawn, with a seat under it, or planting it at the end of a grass walk or paved path. Laburnum shoots and branches are fairly pliable, and it is possible to train them over archways to form a tunnel of blossom above a paved path.

Magnolia

It would be difficult to find a more spectacular and exotic hardy tree than the magnolia, with its glorious white, thickly petalled flowers. Some species are deciduous, some evergreen; they tend to be slow-growing and can be regarded as shrubs when young, and it is many years before they become trees, and even then are rather shrub-like in habit.

Magnolia stellata grows slowly to only about 3.6 m (12 ft), and is much more of a twiggy deciduous shrub, decorated with white flowers. The many, narrow, strap-shaped petals give the blooms a starry appearance on the leafless shoots, to be followed by narrow 10-cm (4-in) long leaves. Their fragrance will scent the air in early–mid spring (see also p.66).

Pittosporum

Pittosporum is usually grown for its glossy light green, undulating leaves which are evergreen, and which cover its tall, shrub-like growth from the ground to its topmost twig. But in the right place, which is a warm, sunny one, it will produce a profusion of small, dark purple-brown flowers, revealing their presence hidden amongst the leaves, by their strong, sweet scent, especially late in the day. Flowering can continue for several weeks.

There are many varieties, several with yellow or white variegated leaves, and all are well worth growing for their ornamental foliage, even if the flowers are only conspicuous by their scent. Provided the soil is medium- to well-drained, they will grow anywhere, but in cool–temperate climates they will need protection from cold wind and prolonged frost. Pruning is unnecessary. A clump of them would make a pretty stand, especially near a pool, and if one is planted close to a house wall, its fragrance will be apparent from inside the house.

Rhododendron

Rhododendrons are *the* shrub to grow in acid soils, and if you want a magnificent display of colour, the hardy hybrids must be the choice. Each bush can be completely covered in trusses of flowers and in many varieties each truss can have twenty flowers in it; so much beauty all at once is difficult to take in. Few, however, are fragrant. A less demanding but scented display is made by the species *R. luteum*, the honeysuckle azalea, whose deep yellow flowers are funnel-shaped, gathered in many-flowered clusters at the end of leafless shoots in late spring. Their intense fragrance gives its presence away many yards from its site and it can continue in flower for three weeks or so.

Its favourite site is light woodland, where it will receive both sun and shade during the day, together with a well-drained soil containing a good deal of rotted organic matter. Height is about 3 m (10 ft).

Skimmia

The rhododendron would make a good background for the low-growing evergreen *Skimmia japonica*, which likes a little shade. The dark green leaves of this

Skimmia × rogersii *rewards its owner with a mass of heavily scented flowers in early spring if given a sheltered, open position.*

Opposite:
On the whole rhododendrons are not scented, but there are some outstanding exceptions, of which the honeysuckle azalea, Rhododendron luteum, *is one.*

90-cm (3-ft) shrub are a foil for the clusters of small white flowers appearing in early to mid spring, but their chief merit is their fragrance, most noticeable if the male form is grown, since this has more flowers than the female, berry-bearing one. Combined with the honeysuckle azalea, it would provide a succession of fragrance and flower, together with an autumn display of orange, red and yellow leaves from the azalea, and large, red, round berries from the skimmia, where both male and female forms are grown. If you can obtain the hybrid *S. × rogersii*, it will be just as well scented as the male form, as well as having a lot of berries, as it is much more free flowering than *S. japonica*.

Lilac

At the end of spring a shrub comes into flower which is more evocative in its fragrance of an English spring than any other: the lilac, although curiously it is not a native of Britain. The common species (*Syringa vulgaris*) is found in the mountains of eastern Europe, but it has been grown in Britain for more than 300 years, and lilacs can be found in village gardens throughout the country.

The modern garden hybrids of this species have large flowerheads, in a great variety of colours. The pale lavender flowers of *S. vulgaris* are, however, strongly scented, and it is the purple, lilac, lavender and mauve hybrids which carry the best scent. Three especially good ones are: 'Andenken an Ludwig Späth', single wine-red; 'Charles Joly', a double deep purple-red, and 'Katherine Havemeyer', also double, coloured lavender-purple. There are many, many more, and it pays to go and see them in flower at a specialist nursery if you can, to establish the degree of fragrance, and to choose precisely the colour you want.

The common species is no problem to grow, doing well on chalky soils and growing in sun or shade, although it flowers better in sun. The habit is rather gaunt, but will be less lanky if the plants are given sufficient space of about 4.5 m (15 ft) between them, and this will result in more flowerheads as well. Prune every two or three years to keep it rounded and not too tall, and do it immediately after flowering.

The hybrids need plenty of sun, a deep alkaline soil and plenty of rotted organic matter as an annual mulch, together with a slow-acting fertilizer in late winter. They should always be dead-headed where possible and practicable; this applies to *S. vulgaris* as well, otherwise they set a great deal of seed and have no energy left over to develop next year's flowers.

These lilacs can become rather tall, large shrubs with a height of 6 m (20 ft); there are some other species and hybrids which are not only lower-growing, but some of which also have a graceful growth habit. The Persian lilac, *S. × persica*, has 7-cm (3-in) long clusters of lilac flowers with a strong perfume on a plant up to 1.8 m (6 ft) tall; *S. sweginzowii* is much more attractive than its name, being about 3 m (10 ft) tall with scented flowers, white inside and pinkish lilac on the outside, towards the end of spring. *S. meyeri* grows to 1.8 m (6 ft) and the deep purple flowers are produced on young plants, in late spring and sometimes again in autumn.

Opposite:
The fragrance of lilacs is typical of spring time, and this hybrid, 'Charles Joly' is one of the sweetest smelling.

Gorse

There is one shrub which not only flowers in spring but in summer and autumn, too, and in winter as well if it is mild enough; in fact, it can easily be in flower in every month of the year. In spite of that, gorse is surprisingly seldom deliberately planted in the garden, all the more surprising in that it is evergreen, and will grow in the poorest soil, provided it is well drained—the more stones the better—and is in a good sunny place. *Ulex europaeus* is really tough, and will withstand all kinds of batterings; it is also formidably spined, so as a hedge it is a super strong barrier. Maybe its very prickliness makes it unpopular, but once planted it need not be handled again, unless it needs shearing, and then leather gloves can be worn to hold shears or long-handled clippers.

The bright golden pea flowers can cover the bush from early to late spring and there will still be some in summer; each bush can grow 60–120 cm (2–4 ft) tall, often taller, and much more in diameter, as it ages. Gorse does particularly well on sunny banks, helping a great deal to prevent soil erosion. If mixed with a planting of the aromatic-leaved *Geranium* 'Johnson's Blue' and either a patchwork of thymes or the prostrate form of rosemary as ground cover, it will provide a fragrant and aromatic planting all year round in what could be a difficult area to plant. There is a smaller species, *U. minor*, which only grows 30 or 60 cm (1 or 2 ft) tall, and flowers later, from mid summer to autumn. It could be interplanted with the tall one if the latter is too large. Gorse flowers smell of a mixture of fruitiness and vanilla, a delicious smell wafting in the spring sunshine and, although it is not this which attracts bees, the flowers will be alive with them as they search out nectar.

Butterflies, like this peacock, are attracted to the tube-like flowers of Buddleia davidii *for the nectar produced at the base of each.*

SUMMER- AND AUTUMN-FLOWERING SHRUBS AND TREES

Abelia
In summer there is a good spread of fragrant flowering shrubs, lasting well into autumn. If you can get the Chinese abelia, *A. chinensis*, to settle down in your garden—it needs warmth and sun, so in cool–temperate climates it must have a south-facing wall—it is not difficult to grow and is impervious to most soil conditions except waterlogging. The small, white, funnel-shaped flowers are pink flushed on the outside, produced in pairs at the tips of the shoots, in later summer and well into autumn, so that their fragrance continues to be a delight for many weeks. A small shrub, 1.5 m (5 ft) tall and as much wide when fully grown, it loses its leaves in winter. No pruning is necessary.

Buddleia
In complete contrast, but flowering at about the same time, is *Buddleia davidii*, the phoenix-like shrub of World War II bomb-sites, which grows easily from seed in Britain, although it is of Chinese origin. Known as the butterfly bush, because of the attraction of its nectar for these beautiful insects, its deep lilac flower spikes unfold in later summer and last for several weeks, with a heavy, honey-like fragrance. There are some exotically coloured hybrids, such as 'Black Knight' whose velvety deep purple spikes are so dark as to be almost black; 'White Profusion', with long, fat spikes, and orange-centred tubular white flowers; 'Empire Blue', almost a true blue with an orange eye; 'Royal Red', whose

very large spikes are red-purple, and 'Harlequin', the reddish purple flowers of which are combined with light green leaves variegated with creamy white.

Height is about 2.4–3 m (8–10 ft), except for 'Harlequin' which grows to about 1.8 m (6 ft), and spread can be 1.8–2.4 m (6–8 ft). They need hard pruning each spring, otherwise they become gaunt and poorly flowered, so should be cut down to about 90–120 cm (3–4 ft). Otherwise they are easily grown in any soil, preferably a sunny place for better flowering, though they will also flower in shade.

Buddleia fallowiana is a particularly pretty species with a white-felted underside to the leaves and similarly fragrant, lavender-coloured spikes of flowers in late summer and autumn. In cool–temperate climates it needs wall protection, and frost may kill it back to the ground, though it will mostly sprout again. Mulching in autumn will help to protect and retain the crown and roots. Height is 1.8 m (6 ft), and it should be pruned down in spring close to ground level.

Calycanthus

The allspices (calycanthus) are not exactly beautiful in flower, but those of the Californian allspice (*C. occidentalis*) have a most unusual fruity, spicy aroma, and the leaves, bark and wood smell of a mixture of camphor and cinnamon. The 7-cm (3-in) wide flowers look like miniature old-fashioned mops, consisting of clusters of strap-shaped petals in varying shades of dull reddish purple tinged with brown, lasting for several weeks, and opening all through summer. Height is about 3 m (10 ft) though it is slow-growing. Eventually the width will be almost

Fig. 6 Calycanthus occidentalis *(Californian allspice)*

as much, with branches close to the soil; it has a tendency to sucker. Its leaves are deciduous, up to 20 cm (8 in) long, varying in shape from rounded to long and narrow. Easily grown, the calycanthus flower best in sun; the soil should be deep and moist, ideally with peat in it. Pruning is unnecessary except occasionally, to remove the oldest branches completely in the spring, to encourage new and better flowering growth.

When the weather is hot and the sun shining, the aroma of this shrub will fill the air with a spicy fragrance. It suits a planting in rough grass, or it can be grown as a specimen in a lawn, provided there is some shelter from other trees and shrubs; its spreading habit can also be made use of to furnish a sunny wall.

Privet

Privet (*Ligustrum ovalifolium*) is virtually never grown except as a formal hedge, and even then is rarely seen at its best, being badly trained and grown in poorly lit sites and starved soils. Given some care and attention, and grown as a specimen evergreen shrub, it is actually most ornamental, with a graceful growth habit, and plumes of white flowers in mid summer on a shrub reaching at least 3.6 m (12 ft). Each cluster can be 10 cm (4 in) long, and has a strong and aromatic smell, redolent of high summer.

Privet has been unnecessarily castigated in the past, probably because it is never grown properly, but it will grow practically anywhere and, being evergreen—except in really severe cold—it is one of the most useful shrubs for hiding utilitarian parts of the garden. The only cutting that need be done is to shape it where required, in early spring, ensuring that the graceful shape is retained.

The golden-leaved form, 'Aureum', whose yellow leaves are green only in the centre, is a distinctive, shorter growing shrub with a looser growth habit; 'Argenteum' has leaves with irregular white leaf margins. Both cultivars provide splashes of light wherever they are grown.

Clerodendrum

The clerodendrums are deciduous shrubs or small trees with the decided asset of flowering in late summer and continuing to do so in early autumn. They grow fast and have large soft, heart-shaped or oval leaves about 23 cm (9 in) long and nearly as wide. In *C. bungei* the flowers are purple-red, in *C. trichotomum* they are white with a red calyx, followed by bright blue pea-like fruit, forming a striking contrast to the calyx; eventually the blue changes to black. In both species the flowers are aromatically fragrant.

Clerodendrum trichotomum can become a small tree at least 3 m (10 ft) tall, but *C. bungei* only reaches about 1.2 or 1.5 m (4 or 5 ft) in cool–temperate climates, although it can grow much taller in warmer regions. The leaves of both species have a strong and unpleasant aroma, but only when bruised or handled. All the members of this genus have scented flowers, but need a good deal of warmth; one of the most fragrant for sub-tropical gardens is *C. fragrans* which has the same spicy perfume as a pink or carnation. The rose-pink flowers are produced in 10-cm (4-in) wide heads in mid to late summer.

These Chinese shrubs are not difficult to grow in most soils and a sunny place with protection from strong wind and cold, but *C. bungei* is often cut down to ground level by cold each winter, regenerating again in spring. *C. trichotomum* needs to be pruned early each spring, cutting the previous year's shoots back to leave only one pair of buds on each. Pruning in this manner will encourage prolific new flowering growth.

Chionanthus

The family *Oleaceae* contains a good many garden plants, all shrubs or small trees, such as lilac, privet, jasmine and also the olive, together with chionanthus, a genus seen not nearly as often as it should be, considering its attractiveness and ease of growth. *C. retusus* is a deciduous shrub from China, whose clusters of strongly-scented white flowers have strap-shaped petals nearly 2 cm (1 in) long. It is early summer-flowering, and can easily be covered by its white flowers, forming a dome-shaped shrub 3 m (10 ft) tall.

Chionanthus virginicus is its American cousin, also a deciduous shrub or small tree 3–9 m (10–30 ft) tall. The feathery clusters of fragrant white flowers which hang down beneath the leaves give it its common name of the fringe-tree; it is not as fragrant as *C. retusus* but is more ornamental, and flowers slightly earlier, in early summer. For both species deep moist soil is important, sun even more so to ripen the new growth for next year's flowering, and to encourage an upright habit. Formal pruning is unnecessary.

Early to mid summer can be a difficult time to find shrubs in flower, after the initial spring burst of forsythia, rhododendrons, camellias and so on, let alone fragrant ones, and the chionanthus are excellent for filling this gap.

Cytisus

Another which flowers in early summer is the pineapple cytisus, *C. battandieri*. This is the genus of the brooms, shrubs generally mildly fragrant; this is one of the most perfumed. It is found growing wild on the Atlas mountains in Morocco, where it grows to 4.6 m (15 ft) and more, although in cultivation height is more likely to be 3–3.6 m (10–12 ft).

Fig. 7 Cytisus battandieri *(pineapple broom)*

It is good value for space because, as well as being fragrant, its pointed decorative leaflets have a silvery sheen all season due to the down which covers them, and bright yellow pea flowers clustered in fat spikes like lambs' tails, about 10 cm (4 in) long, held erect. The fruity pineapple aroma of these is surprising and penetrating. Although it grows quite tall for a shrub, it tends to straggle, and makes the best display where it has a wall or fence to lean against, or where there are brick pillars or wooden posts to which it can be anchored. If its support faces the sun, it will flower at its best, and may set seed in a summer particularly warm for a cool–temperate climate.

As with all the brooms, good soil drainage is essential; it should be pruned back moderately hard when flowering has finished, to remove the oldest shoots, and to encourage new ones to spring up from the base of the plant.

Genista

The genistas are closely related to the brooms and, like them, are mostly without fragrance, but there are two with the same kind of aroma rather than perfume: *G. aetnensis*, and *G. hispanica*.

The Mount Etna broom has yellow flowers with a vanilla odour in mid and late summer, on a tall tree-like shrub at least 4.5 m (15 ft) tall; *G. hispanica*, the Spanish gorse, has fruity, aromatic, deep golden flowers in early summer. Its growth habit is a complete contrast to the Mount Etna broom, as it only grows 45 cm (18 in) tall, and forms a rounded, extremely prickly mound, its brilliant flowers almost completely hiding the framework. The rock-garden is an ideal home for it, and a collection planted in a sunny place will provide a dazzling sheet of colour in summer. Pruning is not necessary, though the Mount Etna broom may need to have straggling shoots removed occasionally, after flowering.

Magnolia

There are some summer-flowering magnolias one of which, *M. grandiflora*, is grand in size as well as in flower, as it can grow to 18 m (60 ft) in the wild, although in cultivation is often only half this height. The heavily fragrant flowers of late summer and autumn are about 25 cm (10 in) wide, a creamy colour, backed by leathery evergreen leaves of a similar length.

Magnolia hypoleuca (syn. *M. obovata*) is an early–mid summer flowering species, its cup-shaped flowers 20 cm (8 in) wide held upright on the somewhat horizontal stems, and strongly scented. The centre contains a 7-cm (3-in) wide conspicuous cluster of purplish red stamens and yellow anthers, which set to produce an equally conspicuous cone-shaped, bright red fruit 20 cm (8 in) long. This Japanese species is an 18-m (60-ft) giant when mature, and is one of the easiest to grow. *M. delavayi* is another late-summer flowering species, less fragrant, but with the merits that it can be accommodated in a smaller space as it is much more shrub-like, and it does not object to an alkaline soil. It has immense evergreen leaves about 34 cm (14 in) long.

These magnolias adapt well to growing against walls which protect them from the north; *M. hypoleuca* is the hardiest of the three—none is tender, but cold winds and frost will brown the flowers, or discourage the buds from opening at all. Giving them the shelter of other trees and shrubs or walls will make a great deal of difference to their flowering display.

Soils should be moist and deep, neutral to acid in reaction, with plenty of rotted organic matter. The time to plant is late spring, when they have started to grow; their fleshy roots are unavoidably damaged at planting time and rot follows, so planting late will ensure that new shoots are easily produced if necessary. Pruning need only be to shape them and keep them under control.

Lime

For large gardens which can accept them, lime trees are well worth growing for the strong honey-like fragrance of their flowers, produced in mid summer, which scents the air all round them for several weeks. Their flowers are particularly popular with bees, and the trees will be swarming with them, producing a constant busy hum through the summer days. The best species to plant is *Tilia* × *euchlora*, because the flowers are particularly well coloured and are especially magnetic to bees—indeed there may be bees on the ground beneath the trees, having absorbed too much nectar, in a temporarily semi-conscious condition.

Height will be about 15 m (50 ft), and it is a graceful tree, well-clothed with drooping branches almost to ground level. The deep creamy yellow flowers form 10-cm (4-in) long clusters, followed by woolly brown fruits. Aphids are a nuisance on other species, as their feeding results in a massive production of sticky honeydew falling on to the ground below, and any objects beneath the trees such as cars, sheds and people, but this tilia will never be infested with them. Cultivation is easy, as most soils and sites suit it.

Myrtle

The myrtle is a very old shrub; that is, it has been deliberately grown for many centuries, because of its striking fragrance; the flowers are perfumed, and the leaves, wood and berries are strongly aromatic. A gum can be obtained from the wood which was thought by the ancient Greeks to smell like myrrh, and oil of myrtle was prized for medicinal uses. *Eau d'ange* is made from the flowers, and the dried berries are still used to flavour food. It is viewed as a symbol of love and kindness, hence the reason for its use at weddings in flower decorations.

Myrtus communis is the species most often grown, thought to have originated in Iran and Afghanistan, and now grown throughout the eastern Mediterranean region. In spite of that, it is hardy in cool–temperate climates, provided it is protected by a south-facing wall, when it will then grow about 3 m (10 ft) tall, clothed in glossy evergreen leaves to ground level. Its white flowers are 2 cm (³/₄-in) wide, with a prominent centre of golden, brushlike stamens, in mid and late summer.

If you have a sheltered but small garden, there is a version of this called *M. c. tarentina* (syn. 'Jenny Reitenbach'), shorter growing to about 1.8 m (6 ft) and with smaller, narrower leaves, and white rather than black, berries. An even smaller version of this is *M. c. t. compacta*.

Cultivation is easy, as the myrtles are not particular about soil, and regular pruning is unnecessary; all they do ask for is sun and warmth.

It must be apparent by now that there are so many shrubs and trees which could be grown for summer scent, a garden full of them could be quite overpowering on a hot day, when the sun's warmth encourages the evaporation of the essential oils. There are three more which no garden should be without, however, and which can scent a garden on their own, so strong is their perfume. Their presence is announced by this invisible quality long before their flowers come into view, so that one might hesitate to add them to a garden which is already well stocked with fragrant plants. The three plants are as follows:

Above: *A hybrid white syringa, which flowers heavily on a moderately sized bush about 1.8 m (6 ft) tall and is heavily perfumed.*

Philadelphus

The mock-orange blossom, also called syringa, which unfortunately confuses it with lilac, flowers in early summer, its four-petalled white flowers heavily fragrant with a perfume reminiscent of orange blossom. *Philadelphus coronarius* is the standard species, a strong and vigorous shrub producing new shoots at least 90 cm (3 ft) long when young in one growing season, the whole plant eventually reaching 3.6 m (12 ft) tall. The specific name is derived from *corona*, meaning a crown, and the flowers were once used in garlands around the head. They have also been used in bridal bouquets as a substitute for orange blossom.

Fortunately there are smaller species, such as 'Belle Etoile', whose 5-cm (2-in) wide flowers have a maroon centre to the creamy white petals, growing to 2 m (6$^{1}/_{2}$ ft); 'Manteau d'Hermine', up to 1.2 m (4 ft) with double white flowers; *P. microphyllus*, about 90 cm (3 ft) tall with small leaves and heavily fragrant white flowers; 'Beauclerk', growing to 1.8 m (6 ft), its 7-cm (3-in) wide flowers have pale pink centres. All of these can become as wide in time as they are high.

They will flower in sun or a little shade; *P. coronarius* is indifferent to most soils, but the smaller ones appreciate good drainage, and are definitely unhappy where the water-table is not far below the surface. Pruning is necessary immediately after flowering, to keep them from becoming crowded, and to encourage flowering comparatively low down. Left unpruned, the large species can overgrow so much as to form tunnels with tall shoots over the top, flowering at the tips. *P. coronarius* is a good species for rough grass, to provide shelter for more tender plants and in a mixed shrub collection separated by grass paths. The small species will fit into borders of herbaceous perennials, providing solidity at the back, or a single specimen could be displayed, planted beside a pool, its green and white colouring adding coolness and tranquillity to the scene.

Honeysuckle

The second of the three with exceptional fragrance is a native of British and European hedgerows, twining amongst them and flowering continuously for most of the summer and autumn. *Lonicera periclymenum*, the honeysuckle or woodbine, was named after a German botanist, Adam Lonicer who lived in the sixteenth century; its specific name is taken directly from the Greek word for honeysuckle, *periklymenon*. Its perfume is at its sweetest on mid summer evenings, permeating the warm air round it for many yards and mingling with the scent of old roses, in flower at the same season.

It is very much a bee plant, and in fact each flower produces an appreciable quantity of sweet, honey-like nectar. A well-grown healthy plant will be covered in these tubular flowers, whose spidery stamens protrude from the end of each bloom; *L. p.* 'Belgica' (Early Dutch) flowers from late spring to mid summer, but in mild seasons or warm gardens, from early spring, its flowers pink or purplish red on the outside. *L. p.* 'Serotina' (Late Dutch) starts in mid summer and carries on until autumn; it is much more yellow than 'Belgica', hardly pink at all. Both climb vigorously, flower within two years of being a rooted cutting, and make a dense mass of growth even more quickly than clematis. There are a lot more honeysuckles with flowers in varying shades of red, orange, yellow and pink-

Opposite:
The fragrance of honeysuckle, Lonicera periclymenum, *is long lasting especially in the evening, when the fragrance spreads far beyond the planting site.*

purple, but some of them are completely unscented and, although pretty flowering climbers, are not, to my mind, worth the name of honeysuckle. However, there is one particularly good one in this group which has bright yellow flowers with the typical fragrance, 'Graham Stuart Thomas', and it flowers from mid summer onwards, so it makes a good variety to pair with the Early Dutch variety.

Fig. 8 Detail of the flower of Lonicera periclymenum *(honeysuckle)*

If you want a wall or fence covered in a hurry, honeysuckles will do the job with the speed of light, but they must have some shade during the day; if planted in the full glare of the sun they become aphid-ridden, mildewy and yellowy green as to foliage, as well as being stunted. They are, after all, plants of hedgerows and light woodland. They do a good clothing job when twining up pillars and pergola posts; they cover 3-m (10-ft) tree stumps effectively, and can be planted at the foot of a living tree which is sparsely branched, such as lilac or rowan.

Climbing honeysuckles can even be formed into a rounded bushy mound, covered with flowers all over it, forming a feature on a lawn, or the centre of a herb garden. Any pruning done is immediately after flowering, to remove some of the flowered growths; the new ones will already be lengthening, and it is on these that flowers will be produced the following year.

Jasmine

There is perhaps no perfume more evocative of a tropical climate than that of the jasmine, a strong and heady fragrance at its most powerful (like honeysuckle) in the evening. It can usually be grown somewhere in a cool–temperate climate garden, whether it is close to a warm south-facing wall or fence, or indoors in the shelter of a cool conservatory. Outdoors, it can easily reach 3.6 m (12 ft) in northern European gardens that have some shelter and sun, especially in town gardens, and will be covered throughout the summer in white tubular flowers, having five petals at the mouth of the tube.

Jasmine is still used to make perfumed garlands and balls of flowers in the countries of the Middle and Far East, and its fragrance is one of the most important in perfume manufacture. *Jasminum officinale* has long been grown in Britain, since at least the middle of the sixteenth century, and probably longer—it could well have been introduced by the Romans, who took their plants with them all over Europe. *J. revolutum* has yellow flowers, also scented, with a longer season lasting until late autumn, but outdoor cultivation is really only for the warmest of cool–temperate gardens.

The jasmines are easy as to soil, provided it is not waterlogged, and pruning need only be done to diminish the tangle of growth, removing the oldest shoots towards the end of the flowering season; it flowers on both previous season's sideshoots and current summer's new growth. In positions it likes it will send up suckers at some distance from the parent plant. As it is another twining climber, it is self-supporting like honeysuckle, so trellis, wire-netting, wires, or simply attaching the stems to nails by wire ties, are all good methods of support. It is ideal for making a bower over an arch.

AUTUMN- AND WINTER-FLOWERING SHRUBS

There is a surprising number of shrubs which flower during this period, and an even more surprising number of them have scented flowers. As is so often the case, the flower colour is not bright, and many are yellow or white—the reason for this colouration is discussed in Chapter One. Nevertheless flowers of any colour are welcome in winter, and the presence of fragrance more than offsets lack of brilliant colour. As with spring- and summer- flowering shrubs and trees, it is possible to have a succession of perfumes from autumn all through winter.

Camellia
Alphabetically, the camellia, *sasanqua*, comes first, flowering in late autumn with small, white, single flowers delicately scented and profusely produced. Trained as an espalier against a sheltered wall, it will have an ephemeral charm in flower; out of flower its evergreen leaves will keep the wall covered all year.

Its hybrids have larger flowers in pink and red as well as white, such as 'Narumi-gata', a large single white with pink edged petals, 'Mine-no-Yuki', white with a peony form, 'Crimson King', a beautiful single bright red, and 'Rosea Plena', loosely double and softly pink-coloured.

Camellias are easy-care shrubs, needing no pruning, and only asking for acid-neutral soil and some shade. In sun the leaves turn a sickly pale yellowish green and if the soil is alkaline, they become bright yellow and cease to grow. *C. sasanqua* and its hybrids must have wall protection in cool-temperate gardens; with this provision they will flower well and regularly.

Chimonanthus
Some of the winter-flowering shrubs are deciduous, some evergreen; the former are of course bare of leaves when they produce their flowers, and one example of this group is the winter sweet, *Chimonanthus praecox*. Its pale yellow, wax-like flowers conceal inner petals of wine-purple, each stalkless flower being produced

An exotic and lingering perfume is a characteristic of Jasminum officinale, *surprisingly hardy in cool-temperate climates.*

Witch-hazel (Hamamelis mollis) _unfolds its spidery petals in mid-winter, but needs to be sniffed to enjoy its perfume._

singly on the stems, and forming almost a bell shape of narrow petals about 3 cm (1 in) long. They are extremely fragrant, flowering most profusely in early winter, but having a flowering period extending from late autumn to early spring.

Chimonanthus was once called calycanthus and is in the same family. It is in fact its Chinese opposite number, with the same long flowering period and strength of perfume, but it is not aromatic as to bark or leaf. It is one of the best winter shrubs for fragrance, though seldom seen, in spite of being quite amenable to alkaline soils. Sun and shelter improve its flowering capacity, and good drainage encourages its rather slow growth to 2.4 m (8 ft), more if close to a wall. Pruning is not required unless it is a wall-grown plant, when it will need crowded and weak growth thinned out in late winter and strong new shoots cut back to half their length.

The winter sweet is quite a large shrub in time, and so perfumes a large area of air, but correspondingly is not for small gardens or spaces.

Daphne

For small gardens you could try *Daphne mezereum*, the mezereon, a strongly scented flowering shrub which is indigenous to Europe including Britain, and thrives on an alkaline soil. It, too, flowers on leafless stems, covering them in cylinders of purple-pink flowers in late winter and early spring. Its mature height is slowly reached at 1.5 m (5 ft) but 90 cm (3 ft) is more likely to be its final height in many cases. Its heavy flowering can be its downfall as it sets so much seed it exhausts itself, so removal of the red berries is worthwhile, particularly as they are poisonous. In a cool, moist, well drained root-run and with shade at some time during the day, it will thrive and be a credit to you. Pruning is not required.

Hamamelis

The witch-hazel, *Hamamelis mollis* is a Chinese shrub slowly growing to 3 m (10 ft) and as much wide, whose leaves are much like those of the hazel or cobnut, but whose flowers are completely different, hence placing it in a different plant family, the *Hamamelidaceae*, rather than the *Corylaceae*. Each flower is a stalkless cluster of spidery golden petals 1.5 cm ($^1/_2$ in) long, on the leafless stems in early-mid winter; the fragrance is there, though it has to be sniffed, and it was some time before I found a specimen whose flowers were fragrant at all. It may be that some clones are not, or that the flowers take time to produce their perfume.

Nevertheless it is another welcome winter-bloomer, and flowers when quite young, only three or four years old. There are many varieties of hamamelis but to ensure they are scented get the hybrids of *H. mollis*, such as 'Goldcrest', centred with wine-purple, or 'Brevipetala', so deep yellow as to appear orange overall; both are strong scented. Another interesting species, more tree-like but with the same flowers, is *H. virginiana*. This blooms from early to late autumn and is similarly fragrant; it is the American counterpart from which the skin lotion (witch-hazel) is made. Soils should be neutral or acid, well-drained and with plenty of organic matter; these shrubs like shelter from wind and sun or some shade. In spite of these requirements they are not difficult to grow—bad drainage is the only real killer—and pruning is unnecessary.

Hamamelis fits into a border well, as the herbaceous perennials round it will need digging up and dividing by the time it has spread to cover them, or it can be grown on its own to decorate a lawn, or be the centre point of an island bed. As with any of these winter shrubs, it pays to plant it where it can easily be seen from the living-room windows.

Mahonia

A particularly good decorative shrub for winter would be one with brightly coloured flowers and evergreen leaves of an interesting shape; one which fits this description is *Mahonia japonica*, which is also what is called an 'architectural' plant, in that its habit of growth is handsome. The glossy evergreen leaves are in feather formation, each leaflet looking like a holly leaf and being nearly as prickly, produced in flat whorls one above the other, and spreading sideways as the shoots divide and branch. The lemon-yellow lily-of-the-valley-like flowers come from the centre of these whorls in loosely spike-like clusters up to 25 cm (10 in) long, from late autumn to late winter, and are heavily fragrant.

It grows quite quickly and does well in light woodland where it is protected from strong and/or cold winds; frost will retard the opening of the flowers but it is otherwise hardy. Rotting organic matter, such as leafmould, regularly added to the soil will keep it in good condition, so that it grows to its full size of 1.8 m (6 ft) and a good deal more wide, but poor soil drainage should be avoided. Pruning is not necessary and indeed is best dispensed with, as mahonia does not take kindly to it; only remove dead growth, in spring.

Mahonia 'Charity' is a hybrid which is also scented, but has an almost tree-like growth habit, with several upright main stems to at least 3 m (10 ft), often much

On a cold winter's day, the fragrance of Viburnum farreri *is an unexpected and welcome addition to the flowers themselves, unusual at this season.*

taller, spreading as wide in time, and with flower spikes over 30 cm (12 in) long, in late autumn and early winter.

Sarcococca

If you have a shaded patch in the garden which is difficult to fill with vegetation other than ferns (and they usually want acid soil), the sweet box is worth trying. *Sarcococca confusa* is an evergreen whose oval pointed leaves, 5 cm (2 in) long, clothe a bush 1.8 m (6 ft) high and wide when fully grown. The tiny clustered flowers are creamy white and are mostly apparent by reason of their fragrance, which scents the air from early to late winter, followed by black berries. It is easily grown in any soil and site, and needs no pruning, so is really rather a good species for a problem corner.

Viburnum

You either like viburnums or find them uninteresting; the genus contains the snowball bush or guelder rose, and laurustinus, a good winter-flowering evergreen, but unfortunately without fragrance. There are some deciduous species with fragrance, a strong one, for instance *V. farreri* (syn. *V. fragrans*). This shrub from northern China will grow 3 m (10 ft) tall and be as wide; from late autumn right through winter into spring it will be in bloom, its tiny flowers in clusters on sideshoots and at the end of shoots. They have a sweet fragrance of heliotrope, guaranteed to pull one up short during a garden meander, whatever the weather, though more than 6°C of frost is likely to damage them. Otherwise the shrub itself is quite hardy. There are two forms, one with pure white flowers called 'Candidissimum', and the species, whose buds are pink-tinged.

An offshoot from *V. farreri* has resulted from a cross between it and *V. grandiflorum*, called *V. × bodnantense*. The variety 'Dawn' is the best one to grow, as it has deep rose pink buds opening to pink tinted flowers, which are more profusely produced than in *V. farreri*, and better able to stand up to frost. The fragrance is as good, but it has rather an ungainly habit, very obvious in winter, and for general garden decoration *V. farreri* is prettier.

Another prettily shaped viburnum is 'Park Farm', a hybrid whose pink-tinted white flowers are the most strongly scented of those mentioned here. Carried in ball-like clusters in spring, their fragrance is almost tangible, acting like a magnet to anyone in their vicinity. Height of this plant is about 2.1–2.4 m (7–8 ft), and it is semi-evergreen.

The viburnums grow easily in most soils, doing best in deep, moist but well drained ones, and a position which gets some sun during the day. The only pruning to do is to cut the oldest shoots right out down to the base in late winter. If the lowest shoots have suckered, these can be removed, too, otherwise it spreads inconveniently.

Clematis

Winter-flowering climbing plants which are fragrant are few and far between, but there are clematis—unusual because even the summer-flowering varieties are not scented—to grow at this season. One is *C. cirrhosa*, and its variety *balearica*. The species flowers from mid winter until early spring, with 6.5-cm (2½-in) wide

Opposite:
A scented clematis is unusual, and this one, C. rehderiana, *is also quite unlike others in the shape of its flowers.*

creamy white flowers, delicately scented, followed by lovely silky, furry seed-heads; its variety, less hardy, has much divided fernlike leaves which become tinted purple and bronze in winter, adding to its decorativeness, while the flowers, also scented and white, last from early autumn to early spring. Although hardy, neither grows more than 1.5 or 1.8 m (5 or 6 ft) in cool–temperate climates, but in warmer regions they can reach 3.6 or 4.5 m (10 or 15 ft).

Clematis flammula only just qualifies for this group, as its flowering starts in late summer, but it then continues into mid autumn. The fragrant white flowers are about 2 cm (1 in) wide, gathered in large clusters about 30 cm (1 ft) long, profusely produced near, and at the top of the plant. It climbs fast to at least 4 m (12 ft), and is a good plant to cover tree stumps or fences, garage or shed walls.

Clematis rehderiana is another clematis flowering at the same two seasons but it has quite different flowers in that they are pale yellow, bell-shaped and hang down in their rather upright clusters. Their fragrance is said to be like that of cowslips, though I find it to be simply sweet and flowery. This is a vigorous species forming curtains of foliage and flowers, and easily able to swarm up to 6 m (20 ft) if given the opportunity.

Pruning of *C. cirrhosa* and its variety is hardly needed except to cut out dead shoots and reduce the tangle a little each year in spring. The other two can be left alone, though flowering will then diminish gradually, and they are better cut back hard to within 90 cm (3 ft) of the ground in late winter, so that they produce plenty of new flowering shoots early in the year. Clematis will grow in most soils and sun with some shade.

Honeysuckle

There is one good winter-flowering honeysuckle which is scented; this is *Lonicera fragrantissima*, evergreen in mild gardens, and producing the typical honeysuckle-shaped flowers between mid winter and early spring. It is a bushy species, not a climber, forming a rounded mound with age, eventually about 2.1 m (7 ft) high, with pairs of its creamy white flowers evenly carried all over it. Pruning is hardly necessary except to remove some of the oldest shoots, in spring.

AROMATIC FOLIAGE AND BARK

It is a moot point whether 'aromatic' shrubs and trees can be included in a book about 'fragrant' species, but since they are pleasant to inhale, they are worth mentioning, if only briefly. Herbal aromas will be described in Chapter Seven.

Callistemon

Callistemon citrinus, the bottlebrush plant, has leaves smelling vividly of lemon when bruised; its red flowers appear in summer on a bush up to 4.5 m (15 ft) tall in its native Australia, but only half this height in cool–temperate climates, where it needs sun and good drainage close to a wall to survive.

Cistus

Some of the cistus (rock roses) species give off their strong aromas freely in the heat of the sun in summer. *C. × ladanifer* is the gum cistus, growing about 1.2 m (4 ft) high and wide, with large, white, saucer-shaped 10 cm (4 in) flowers, blotched centrally with deep red; *C. × cyprius* is larger, growing to 1.8 m (6 ft), with smaller but similarly coloured flowers, and is hardier, surviving all but really severe winters. Both have sticky aromatic leaves and flower in early summer. *C. laurifolius* is a similar height, but with plain white flowers all summer, and heavily aromatic leaves smelling of incense. It is hardy. The ladanum obtained from the leaves is used as one of the bases for perfumes, and the purest is said to come from *C. × cyprius*.

If planted in a sunny place and, preferably, stony soil, these cistus will give off an authentic aroma of the Mediterranean hillsides in summer, especially if mingled with thyme and marjoram; they are ideal for a rock garden, and need little care, beyond deadheading; pruning is unnecessary.

Eucalyptus

Eucalypts have highly aromatic foliage, and in *Eucalyptus globulus* the aroma is of the oil so often recommended for medicinal use in coughs and colds. *E. gunnii* is pungently and refreshingly aromatic, and it can be grown as a tree, or as a shrub, by cutting it down practically to ground level every spring. As a tree it will grow fast in one season, as much as 1.8 m (6 ft), and will have a white to grey bark, and silvery blue, round leaves while young; later come pointed, long, grey-green leaves. It needs shelter from wind to prevent it blowing over, and prolonged cold wind will kill it; most soils are suitable except shallow alkaline ones. It is the best to grow in cool–temperate climates, though *E. globulus* will survive in really mild, sheltered gardens of such climates, making a large tree up to 30 m (100 ft) and more.

Bog myrtle

In complete contrast the bog myrtle (*Myrica gale*) grows to about 90 cm (3 ft), usually much less in its natural habitat of bogs. It is a deciduous bushy little shrub whose shining green leaves have a strong sweet aroma when crushed; when dried they were once used for scenting sheets and other household linen. Its wood is also aromatic, its flowers are greenish yellow catkins produced in late spring and early summer. It is hardy and native to the northern hemisphere including Britain, so needs no special cultural treatment.

Poplar

The balsam poplars are deservedly renowned for their aromatic buds and leaves. As they unfold and develop in spring, the air is filled with their spicy smell, and the garden that contains a specimen will always be remembered. *Populus trichocarpa* is the most handsome, and the best form to obtain is 'Fritzi Pauley', as it is resistant to bacterial canker, the scourge of its progenitor and other balsam poplars. It is a large tree, to at least 30 m (100 ft) with large, pointed leaves up to 18 cm (7 in) long; the female catkins can be 15 cm (6 in) long. The trees grow rapidly and do best in deep moist soils; their wide-spreading roots can cause damage to house foundations and drains, particularly in heavy soils, if planted nearby. They need plenty of space wherever they are grown, and are in fact at their most decorative if planted as specimens.

CHAPTER SIX

THE ROSARIE

'Roses, damask and red, are fast flowers of their smells; so that you may walk by a whole row of them, and find nothing of their sweetness; yea, though it be in a morning's dew.' Reluctantly it has to be admitted that Francis Bacon was right when he thus remarked in his essay *Of Gardens*, but although the fragrance of old roses is unlikely to scent the surrounding air, that of modern hybrids is, especially the single- and cluster-flowered ones. Nevertheless, the old shrub roses have a powerful fragrance if you bury your face in a bloom and the rose perfume lasts well through repeated sniffings, being refreshing and sweet, but not overly so; some varieties have fruity overtones.

Rose-water, in spite of its name, does not smell much like the flower fragrance, mainly because that fragrance is made up of 12 different substances, only one of which will dissolve to any degree in water. However, rose-water still manages to smell delicious. The oil, or attar of roses, contains the remaining 11, some of which are: nerol, also found in orange-blossom and wallflower; farnesol, in lily-of-the-valley and mignonette, and linalool, in lavender and jonquil. Substances also figure in the rose perfume make-up which are found in mint, caraway, geranium and eucalyptus.

Any rose which is perfumed always has a delightful scent, and the range of perfumes is greater than with any other flower. It was suggested in 1885 that there were 17 different fragrances and, when you consider the 11 constituents mentioned earlier, the odours of the other flowers in which they are contained, and the fact that they can all be combined differently through hybridizing, it is not surprising that 25 were found in an American rose garden in 1962, and it is more than likely that this is still only a few of the rose's odours. Violet, lemon, clove, banana and apple are additional scents to that of the typical rose perfume as found in the petals of the Kazanluk roses, *Rosa damascena trigintipetala*, which are used to make the best attar of roses. *R. alba* is also used, but its attar is less good.

The beginning of the rose's history and its association with mankind is lost in the mists of antiquity:

> *No man knows,*
> *Through what wild centuries,*
> *Roves back the Rose*

but since some roses, notably *R. chinensis* and *R. gigantea*, grow wild in China, it is certain that the Chinese appreciated it and cultivated it for its beauty and fragrance. The Persian rose, *R. foetida persiana*, is a Middle Eastern rose; some have their origin in India and the Egyptians dedicated roses to their gods. As civilization followed civilization, the rose must have been carried westwards until it arrived in Greece, when Herodotus in the fifth century BC wrote of the damask rose that it had 'a scent surpassing all others'.

All the classic Roman writers praised the rose for its perfume, and Pliny said that: 'the Isle of Albion (Britain) is so called from its white cliffs washed by the sea or from the white roses with which it abounds', possibly *R. canina*, the dog rose, which is sometimes white, or such a pale pink as to appear white.

Rhodes—the Greek island—is thought to derive its name from the red roses grown there for the Romans, who went overboard about roses and their fragrance in the way that the Dutch did for tulips in the seventeenth century. They made wine out of them; used them in medicine, and used the petals to carpet banqueting halls—the thicker they were, the wealthier the host. They were used to fill pillows, and worn by the army when it went to war; rose-water was used for bathing in.

The Romans would have been responsible for disseminating the rose throughout Europe, and taking it across the water to Britain, and it must have continued to be popular throughout the Dark Ages, somehow being grown in monastery gardens and the gardens of the wealthy in spite of the unsettled times. During mediaeval days, there were three roses which were preferred above any others: *R. alba*, *R. damascena* and *R. gallica*. All three are still available and grown today.

OLD ROSES

Rosa alba

The white rose (*R. alba*) was a Roman rose, and it was adopted by the Yorkists at the time of the Wars of the Roses in Britain so that it came to be called the White Rose of York. Today's authorities regard this double, single or semi-double, scented white rose as a hybrid rather than a species. Height is between 1.2 and 2.4 m (4 and 8 ft), and the leaves are blue-grey, while the thorns are few. Flowering is in early to mid summer.

Rosa damascena

Rosa damascena, the Damask rose, named after the city of Damascus (although it is also said that Damascus was named after the rose) may have been distributed through Europe and Britain by the Crusaders. It is more than likely a hybrid rather than a species, which would account for its variability of colour from white through pink to rose-red, but whatever its botanical status is, it is a large, exceptionally fragrant, double rose, blooming from early to mid summer. It grows naturally in the Balkans, and its variety *trigintipetala* is used there for making attar of roses. Height is 90–150cm (3–5 ft). Its variety (or hybrid) *bifera*, the autumn damask, flowers twice, in autumn as well as summer, and is equally fragrant. The 'York and Lancaster' rose, also fragrant, is a damask rose with flowers striped and blotched pink or rose on a white ground, less free-flowering, and growing up to 2.4 m (8 ft).

Rosa gallica

One of the oldest of the old shrub roses is *R. gallica officinalis*, the apothecary's rose of Provins. Its flowers are double, deep crimson with a central boss of golden stamens, and its thick petals have an intensely strong perfume which lasts even when they are dried and crushed to powder. Because of this property it was used to make confections and preserves of roses, and it is of course still a marvellous rose for making pot pourri. There are a number of hybrids, of which *R. g. versicolor* ('Rosa Mundi') is probably the most well-known for its striking colouring of crimson striped and marked with light pink.

'Tuscany Superb', another gallica hybrid, is a beautiful colour, rich deep velvety wine-purple, with a formal flat, double flower filled with golden stamens in the centre, and having a sweet fragrance. 'Belle de Crecy' is better than 'Tuscany Superb' for fragrance and is one of the best of the old roses in this respect, with flat, double flowers, almost magenta coloured, changing to violet.

Height of all these gallica roses—there are many more—is 90–120 cm (3–4 ft), with one summer blooming only, but their fragrance and beauty is exceptional. *R. g. versicolor* in particular makes an outstanding display, and has the merit of remaining compact, making it a good shrub for gardens where space is at a premium.

Rosa centifolia

The old cabbage rose, *R. centifolia*, is another one from the mountainous regions of the Balkans, right across to Iran, in spite of which its alternative common name is the Provence rose. Its flowers are very large and double, a pure rose-pink, powerfully scented and carried on stems which arch over; indeed the whole habit of the 1.5-m (5-ft) bush is graceful and arching, festooned with its voluptuous flowers, sometimes clustered, sometimes carried singly.

One of the most fragrant and striking hybrids of the cabbage rose is 'Tour de Malakoff', averaging 1.5–1.8 m (5–6 ft). The very large 10–12-cm (4–5-in) blooms are crimson-red as they unfold, streaked with violet, the underside of the petals being a much paler mauvy pink. As it matures, the colouring changes to deep purple, finally lightening to grey and lilac. It needs a good strong soil to do it justice.

'Fantin Latour' is a similar height but quite a different colour as to flower, since the rounded blooms are an exquisite delicate shell-pink—a greater contrast could not be imagined. The centre is a deeper rose-pink, and the whole flower has the characteristic fragrance of the species.

If you have room for only one more of these cabbage roses, 'Robert le Diable' would fill the space best. It flowers late, in mid summer, is not so tall, at about 1.2 m (4 ft), and has blooms which could be the forerunner of the pointed, large-flowered (hybrid tea) roses, since the centre petals are upright and curve round one another, while the outer ones turn outwards and downwards. Its colouring is

Opposite:
This red and white rose is a damask rose called 'York and Lancaster' with the typical strong fragrance of its type.

on the same lines as 'Tour de Malakoff', but if anything, is even more exotic, starting with deep purple and showing all shades of this, together with wine, magenta, lilac, red and finally grey, so that a mixture of blooms on a bush is a tremendous eye-catcher.

Cultivation of old shrub roses

I cannot help feeling that much the best way to grow the old shrub roses is in grass, though the standard advice is to plant them in borders, preferably with a wall backing them. They are big plants, 1.2–2.4 m (4–8 ft) tall, and easily 1.8 m (6 ft) wide. Of the taller kinds, one of these is quite large enough to be a specimen on its own, and a group of three of the smaller ones is just as pretty a planting. Memories of the moss roses in my childhood home are of showers of crimson petals on the grass surrounding them, and great, full-blown blooms arching over after rain, almost down to the turf.

Grown like this they have a chance to develop their full spread, and can be enjoyed on all sides. Above all, they are not crowded; if you cram a lot of old roses into a small space, not only is the resultant picture confusing, but their loose and informal growth habit becomes tangled and restricted. You could compromise by growing them in beds with wide grass paths between them, but however you grow them, do give them the space they need.

Blending the colours should not be a problem, since practically all are shades of pink, red, crimson, purple, magenta, with the occasional white or salmon-pink. The only yellow one is *R. hemisphaerica* (syn. *R. sulphurea*), a golden globe of a bloom, which forms the subject of one of Redouté's best paintings. Although like a centifolia flower and once known as the Yellow Provence, it is not truly that species, and flowers best in warm climates.

Bourbon roses

One of my favourite groups of old roses is the Bourbon collection, the bourboniana hybrids, perhaps not strictly speaking a really old rose, since the first one was born of a natural cross in 1817. This was between 'Parson's Pink China' and the pink 'Autumn Damask' on the island of Bourbon, near Mauritius, off the east coast of Madagascar. They have one outstanding merit that the older shrub roses, apart from the Autumn Damask or the Quatre Saisons rose, do not: that of repeat flowering, in autumn as well as in summer, and it was this characteristic which was bred into the hybrid perpetuals and eventually our modern hybrid teas, now called large-flowered shrub roses.

In fact, they flower in between as well, though not as freely, but they can justifiably be said to be perpetual-flowering. Besides this, they are heavily fragrant, and the flat-faced but rounded flowers are 'quartered', that is, the tightly packed petals are in whorls, usually four, one in each quarter, sometimes with a central green 'button'. The original hybrid has reddish pink flowers with the damask fragrance; later hybrids ranged through all the rose colours except yellow, from white to deep crimson.

Opposite:
'Zephirine Drouhin' is a semi-climbing Bourbon hybrid, whose stems are virtually thornless and which flowers all summer.

The Bourbons like sun and warmth and, given these two conditions and a decent soil, they make a glorious and perfumed show all summer. One of the most fragrant is 'Variegata di Bologna', also one of the strongest, growing to 2.4 m (8 ft), with wall protection. It is one of the stripey roses, with virtually white petals streaked deep crimson to black, forming a quartered, globular bloom.

'Commandant Beaurepaire' is another eye-catching striped job, its ball-like flowers coloured purple, red, pink, maroon and rose, also very well scented. At mid summer it flowers profusely, less so in autumn than its relatives. 'Souvenir de la Malmaison' was one of the earliest hybrids to be produced, in 1843, and is a big rose, reaching up to at least 3 m (10 ft), with a circumference to match. The familiar globular quartered flowers are large, 10–12 cm (4–5 in) wide, and flesh pink in colour, strongly and unusually scented. It flowers as well in autumn as in summer.

The best known of these Bourbons is 'Zéphirine Drouhin', produced in 1868. Some call it a climber, but it is more often a large and sprawling bush which can be trained flat against a wall or along a trellis fence to a length of 3 m (10 ft), sometimes more. Its blooms are heavily scented, and it can be in flower in late spring, continuing right through into mid autumn. The colour is a bright carmine pink and the flower shape is open and flattish, semi-double. A further bonus is its thornless character.

Moss roses

At the end of the seventeenth century, a rose appeared in the south of France amongst a group of *R. centifolia*, which had a great deal of what looked like coarse green fur on the outside of the flower buds, on the flower stems and even on the leaves. The flowers were ball-shaped and clear pink, and the plant grew eventually to about 1.2 m (4 ft) tall. Known either as *R. centifolia muscosa* or *R. muscosa*, the moss rose probably appeared as a result of a mutation, and has retained the fragrance of its progenitor.

Moss roses were popular with the Victorians, and there were once more than fifty hybrids, all with scented flowers; even the moss has an aroma, mostly of balsam. The scent in the flowers comes from the central style, rather than the petals, and may explain why it is so penetrating. There is a white form of the original called *alba* which is faintly pink-tinted in the centre just as it opens, but this quickly fades; it is very fragrant and beautifully mossed. 'Gloire des Mousseux' has the largest flowers, clear pink and rounded, with light green moss which perfectly complements the shade of pink.

The moss roses are characteristically shades of pink, reds and purples, but 'Golden Moss', a modern hybrid, is golden-yellow, opening from pale orange buds. 'Nuits de Young' is a complete contrast, its small flowers being such a deep velvety purple as to be virtually black, with a centre of golden stamens. 'William Lobb' is one of the most fragrant, and a large shrub to 2.4 m (8 ft) tall, whose semi-double flowers range through crimson, purple, lilac and grey as they mature and fade. There are many more hybrids, but those mentioned give a range of the moss rose colouring and habit. As with the centifolias, they are once-flowering in mid summer.

Musk roses

If any rose is likely to be fragrant, it has to be one with the specific name of *moschata*. The musk roses did actually find favour with Francis Bacon, unlike the

Fig. 9 Rosa centifolia muscosa *(moss rose)*

damask and 'red' (gallica) varieties, as he described their fragrances as being next to the violet: 'which above all others yields the sweetest smell in the air'. The flowers of *R. moschata* are a creamy white, single, and about 5 cm (2 in) wide, and their fragrance is delicious and strong. You need a large garden or a tall tree, as it is an exceedingly vigorous climber, to 12 m (40 ft), and you may find it more convenient to grow one of the hybrids descended from it, bred by the Rev. Pemberton early this century and known as the Hybrid Musks. Their ancestry is very mixed, and *R. moschata* is about eight generations removed, but the perfume is still strong in the hybrids.

They bloom from early summer into autumn; either grow them as single specimens in grass, or line them up to make an informal flowering hedge, about 1.2 m (4 ft) tall, but allow a width of at least 1.5 m (5 ft) if you use them in this way. Amongst the best are: 'Cornelia', deep to light pink; 'Felicia', peach-pink, my own favourite; 'Moonlight', pale yellow to white, bronze young leaves; 'Penelope', a pale salmon-pink fading to creamy white. Keep deadheading them to encourage continued flowering, and keep an eye open for mildew as the summer advances.

A scented rose hedge is an outstanding feature, and to create it a musk rose hybrid, such as 'Felicia', is perfect.

Other Old Climbing Roses

Another species which has contributed a unique fragrance to roses is *R. gigantea*, the wild tea rose. It, too, is a climber to 12 m (40 ft), whose flowers are light yellow or white, produced early, in late spring and early summer. The so-called tea scent is arguable, some maintaining that there is no trace of it in the perfume, others that the tea smell is similar to the dried leaves or to freshly brewed tea; some say that the plants smell of tea through being shipped in tea chests. Whatever it is, it is supposed to have been bred into the modern large-flowered (hybrid tea) roses, some of which are unscented, and some of which have a considerable range of perfumes including fruity ones. 'Hume's Blush Tea-scented' rose now called *Rosa odorata* 'Odorata' is one of the most famous hybrids from it, with small double, light pink flowers. 'Park's Yellow Tea-scented China' has much larger, bright yellow flowers with thick petals, and introduced a complete change of colour into the race. Its name is now *Rosa odorata* 'Ochroleuca'.

The old climbing roses vary considerably in the height to which they can climb, and some of them look their best if they have 9-m (30-ft) trees to scramble over and eventually hang down in a curtain of scented colour. Others are less exuberant as to growth, though perhaps even more floriferous.

If you train the tawny yellow 'Gloire de Dijon' against a sunny wall, it will need 4.5 m (15 ft) of space each way, and nearly as much in height. House walls could cramp its style, but a boundary wall facing south would suit, or a garage or stable wall of brick or stone.

There are smaller climbers which restrict themselves to a mere 3–3.6 m (10–12 ft); they can be trained up single supports such as brick pillars, wooden poles or arches, of which there are now some most attractive ones copying the gothic-shaped arch so popular with the Victorians. A series of arches forming a tunnel makes a very good ornamental feature, especially if perpetual flowering climbers are used, and of course the planting need not consist solely of roses. It can be mixed with all sorts of other climbers—honeysuckle with apricot-pink 'Compassion', summer jasmine with 'Climbing Lady Sylvia' or 'Zéphirine Drouhin', or the pale yellow *Clematis rehderiana* with 'Gloire de Dijon'.

The more vigorous climbers can be coaxed along supports between pillars or poles, so that they form swags of bloom on swinging loops of chain or rope like ship's hawsers. Or try the time-honoured ways of growing climbing roses over porches and round front-doors, or forming bowers and arbours in sunny corners of the garden.

While we are on the subject of climbers, one of the prettiest and most fragrant is *R. banksiae alba*, with small white, double flowers profusely produced, on a plant climbing to 6 m (20 ft) and more. 'Lutea' has pale yellow flowers, even more charming and looking like double primroses; both are almost evergreen. With a sunny south-facing wall in cool–temperate climates, either will flower in late spring, earlier in warmer countries.

Another gloriously scented old climber is *R. banksiae* 'Kiftsgate', its clusters of white, single flowers profusely produced in mid summer, whatever the climate. It climbs to 9 m (30 ft) and more, and will hang like a waterfall of bloom from trees. Your nose will always tell you that it is in the vicinity, long before you see it.

'Gloire de Dijon' is an old climbing tea rose introduced in 1853, and still popular for its large, deep buff-yellow flowers, one of the best climbers for perfume, and having the added asset of flowering from early summer until early autumn. It will need 4.5 m (15 ft) of space, but be careful to buy it from a good rose specialist

Fig. 10 *Chimonanthus praecox.*

as there are some stocks about which are weak. Mildew can sometimes be a problem. This is a Noisette Climber—Philippe Noisette was a nurseryman in Charleston, South Carolina, working with roses, with the help of his brother in France, during the last century.

'Mme Alfred Carrière' is another Noisette climber, introduced about thirty years later, having large, double, white flowers flushed pink, with musky fragrance. It is extremely hardy, flowers all summer and into autumn, and will flower even if its support faces north and never gets the sun.

Fragrant leaves

All the fragrance so far discussed comes from the flowers of roses, and in practically all the species the leaves are completely scentless. However, there is one which is outstanding for its leaf aroma, and that is the eglantine of Shakespearean fame: 'I know a bank whereon the wild thyme blows . . . Quite over-canopied . . . with sweet musk roses and with eglantine.' *Rosa eglanteria* is the sweetbrier, whose leaves smell so strongly of apple when rubbed, and even without rubbing after a summer shower. Its single flowers are light pink, on a strong growing, very prickly plant 2.1 m (7 ft) tall.

The sweetbrier was used in the 1890s by Lord Penzance to produce a race of scented-leaved hybrids in different colours than pink. 'Lady Penzance' has large copper-rose flowers with prominent golden stamens; 'Lord Penzance' has flowers in fawn, pink and yellow, fragrant as well as the leaves; 'Amy Robsart' is deep rose-pink; 'Jeannie Deans' is brilliant scarlet, 'Lucy Ashton' is white with a pink edge. All are mid summer flowering, but not for long, and about 1.5–1.8m (5–6 ft) tall; they do well as hedges.

MODERN ROSES

No chapter on roses can leave out the modern hybrids and, in spite of a general belief that they have no perfume, there are actually a good many with a strong perfume, one which scents the air and is not merely carried within the bloom; also of course, the shape of the modern large-flowered hybrids (hybrid teas) is superb; even the blooms of the cluster-flowered hybrids (floribundas) are tending to become larger and more classically pointed in shape. If you are critical, you could describe the old rose flowers as being unformed, untidy and messy!

The modern roses, too, all have the ability to flower continuously really well all summer and well into autumn, even during early winter if the garden or the weather is suitably mild in cool–temperate climates. In spite of the dictum that their habit is stiff and unprepossessing, especially out of flower, when they are in leaf and bloom, they are perfectly presentable, provided they are grown well. They need plenty of rotted organic matter each year, as a mulch, and feeding in early summer to produce good, glossy, well coloured foliage, and strongly held blooms which last well. Good pruning is vital, together with regular deadheading.

Plants to grow with roses

Instead of growing roses in solid blocks, in beds and borders, why not mix them with other plants? Shrubs for instance, which flower at different times, or coincide with them, such as *Skimmia × rogersii* or the lovely Mexican orange blossom (choisya), both spring-flowering; lavender, the smaller philadelphus hybrids, or buddleia in late summer. Some of these are evergreen and will help to clothe the nakedness of the roses in winter. The silverberry, *Elaeagnus commutata*, could provide a singular combination of colour with the right roses, 'Blue Moon' perhaps, or 'Alec's Red' to contrast rather than blend.

Perennials could nestle round their ankles such as the delicately scented polyanthus and primulas, or wallflowers, which can last from year to year in mild climates, and flower just before the roses. Border carnations and pinks are low growing and evergrey, good for the front of roses, violets are another early flowerer, and sweet rocket can grow up amongst them, adding its strong fragrance to theirs.

Rue and hyssop are good herbs for combining with modern roses; they both soften their winter appearance by being evergreen, and the rue is particularly attractive in the cultivar 'Jackman's Blue', its filigree leaves lasting all year. The coloured-leaf salvias, too, are neat small bushes, their varied leaf colours providing a suitable blend for any of the roses, whether you plant 'Icterina' with yellow-edged foliage, 'Purpurascens' with a purple flush or 'Tricolor' whose grey-green leaves are white-edged and pink-tinted.

An island bed planted with a mixture of plant types which includes modern roses makes the best of all worlds, and the rose in such surroundings can compete with the lily as the queen of the garden. The same applies to a mixed border; a modern rose will never look out of place, provided there are other shrubs in the border, and there is a range of heights amongst all the plants. A one-colour border works well, too, such as a red or yellow one—the single colour helps the rose to fit in and avoid being conspicuous.

'Wendy Cussons' is a large-flowered (hybrid tea) rose with one of the most powerful fragrances of any rose.

'Whisky Mac' makes an excellent patio rose as it flowers heavily on a low-growing bush, is an unusual colour, and is strongly scented.

'Arthur Bell' is a cluster-flowered (floribunda) hybrid, strong growing and with one of the most typical of the rose perfumes.

'English Miss' is consistently one of the most popular of the scented cluster-flowered (floribunda) hybrid roses.

Hybrid rose types

There are many hybrids and the following lists are only the tip of the iceberg, to provide a basis from which to work.

Scented large-flowered (hybrid tea) roses

Name	Colour	Height in cm(in)
'Alec's Red'	red	90(36) plus
'Alpine Sunset'	yellow and pink	60–90(24–36)
'Admiral Rodney'	pink	90(36) plus
'Blue Parfum'	purple-grey	90(36) plus
'Deep Secret'	dark red	60–90(24–36)
'Double Delight'	red and white	60–90(24–36)
'E.H. Morse'	red	90(36) plus
'Fragrant Cloud'	red	60–90(24–36)
'Fragrant Dream'	apricot	90(36) plus
'Fragrant Gold'	deep yellow	60–90(24–36)
'Incense'	red	90(36) plus
'John Waterer'	dark red	60–90(24–36)
'Just Joey'	orange-copper	60–90(24–36)
'Lady Sylvia'	salmon-pink	30–60(12–24)
'Mala Rubenstein'	salmon-pink	60–90(24–36)
'My Choice'	pink and yellow	90(36) plus
'Rebecca Claire'	copper and coral	60–90(24–36)
'Silver Lining'	pink	60–90(24–36)
'Snow White'	white	90(36) plus
'Typhoo Tea'	cerise and cream	90(36) plus
'Velvet Fragrance'	deep crimson	60–90(24–36)
'Wendy Cussons'	rose red	90(36) plus
'Whisky Mac'	gold, orange and copper	30–60(12–24)

Scented cluster-flowered (floribunda) roses

Name	Colour	Height in cm(in)
'Amberlight'	brown	
'Arthur Bell'	yellow	
'Beauty Queen'	pink	
'Champagne Cocktail'	yellow	
'Dearest'	pink	
'Elizabeth of Glamis'	salmon-pink	
'English Miss'	pink	
'Fragrant Delight'	copper-pink	
'Iced Ginger'	yellow and white	all are 60–90(24–36)
'Margaret Merrill'	white	
'Magenta'	lilac	
'Orange Sensation'	orange	
'Rosemary Rose'	rose-red	
'Salmon Sprite'	salmon-pink	
'Shocking Blue'	magenta	
'Sheila's Perfume'	yellow and red	

'Dearest' is an enchanting rose, both in colour and perfume.

For fragrance 'Margaret Merril' is hard to beat, and is another in the top ten of favourite roses.

'Albertine' produces a glorious show for about three weeks in early to mid-summer, with a delicate scent in the heart of each shell-pink flower.

Patio and miniature roses

If you are an ardent rosarian and you are short of gardening space, there are smaller roses, the so-called patio roses of about 45 cm (18 in) in height, and the real miniatures 15–30 cm (6–12 in) tall, with tiny flowers. They do very well in beds bordering the patio, or planted in spaces in the paving or decking, or grown in containers. Like their larger relatives, these small roses combine well with other plants, mignonette or lily-of-the-valley, knee-high sweetpeas, hyacinths or cistus (the rock-rose), or the small version of myrtle, *Myrtus communis tarentina*.

Patio and miniature scented roses

Name	Colour	Height in cm(in)
'Cider Cup'	apricot	45(18)
'Dwarf King'	red	20(8)
'Gingernut'	bronze	45(18)
'Gold Pin'	yellow	30(12)
'Red Ace'	deep red	20–30(8–12)
'Sweet Fairy'	lilac-pink	15(6)
'Sweet Magic'	orange and gold	38(15)

Climbing Roses

'Albertine' looks like one of the old climbing roses, but is actually a modern one of the Wichuriana type, introduced in 1921. It is extremely vigorous, especially in a well broken-down heavy soil, and needs considerable pruning to keep it under control, wearing leather gloves, as its thorns are large and painful. It flowers profusely, in shades of salmon and coppery pink opening from carmine buds, and remains in flower for about a month, from early to mid summer, smelling sweetly and strongly.

Following it came 'Mme Grégoire Staechelin', in 1927, a pretty, large-flowered climber, with coral-pink, frilled petals, heavily scented and as profusely produced as those of 'Albertine', for the same length of time; it, too, needs considerable pruning, and stands up well to severe weather.

Amongst the modern climbers, one of the best is 'Compassion', from the Harkness stable, with apricot-pink double flowers, beautifully scented; it is not over-vigorous, to about 3 or 3.6 m (10 or 12 ft), and is well suited to training on a pillar. 'Crimson Glory' is a hybrid tea type, a climbing sport from the bush, introduced during World War II. The deep crimson flowers are velvety in texture, and its fragrance is outstanding. Added to that is its uninhibited flowering all summer, so that it can be forgiven for its tendency to be infested with mildew. Height is about 4.5 m (15 ft).

For a complete contrast in colour, choose 'Climbing Lady Sylvia', a pastel pink and yellow, a charming rose with a strong perfume, growing strongly to about 6 m (20 ft). This is a between-wars sport from the bush form, which was itself a sport from 'Mme Butterfly' (1918), in turn sporting from 'Ophelia' in 1912, when the lineage ends—parentage of this is unknown. It has comparatively few thorns. Pruning should not be too hard to obtain the best flower display.

Cultivation of modern roses

Rose cultivation in general is much the same as that for other flowering shrubs, though perhaps the large-flowered and cluster-flowered hybrids need more attention to feeding and mulching, and to deadheading in particular. The two main disease problems are mildew and black spot, but many now have disease resistance built into them by their breeders, particularly with regard to black spot. Mildew infection is often a sign that the plants require airier conditions, and more water at the roots, hence the need to water climbing roses against walls and fences regularly in dry weather, and to maintain a gap between their growth and the wall behind them.

As regards pruning, the large single-flowered (hybrid tea) types need to be cut down when planted, to leave stems a few centimetres long, with two or three dormant buds on each stem. Mature plants need to be cut back early each spring so as to leave the bush about half the height it was before pruning.

Cluster-flowered (floribunda) hybrids also need to be cut back hard to leave about 15 cm (6 in) of stem immediately after planting. Mature plants are pruned so that one, or perhaps two, of the oldest shoots are cut back to ground level; the youngest growth is cut by about a quarter of its length, and the remainder by about half.

Climbers are of two types: ramblers and climbers. The type of climber will be very apparent by the way it produces new shoots, either very long ones from the base, or much shorter ones from the existing stems. The ramblers have all their flowered growth cut out at ground level, and the new stems tied in in their place, either in autumn or early spring. The climbers are generally cut very little, merely removing flowered growth, and cutting back sideshoots produced on new stems, to leave a stem with one or two buds on it; this also can be done in autumn or early spring.

Patio roses can be treated like small versions of the cluster-flowered hybrids. Miniatures hardly need any pruning, beyond shaping them, and for really dwarf ones, this is best done with nail scissors.

More information on general cultivation will be found in Chapter Ten at the end of the book.

CHAPTER SEVEN

HERBAL FRAGRANCE AND AROMA

No garden intended to smell delicious should be without herbs. Indeed, no garden intended to be ornamental should be without them, although some of the most decorative varieties are not the most fragrant or aromatic. In general this group of plants has the most to contribute to a garden in the way of spicy aromas. Quite often, these are a hidden asset; a herb's leaves need to be rubbed or crushed to break the minute oil glands, and to release their often nose-tickling scent, unlike the perfume of many flowers, which is released naturally into the air. This characteristic can dictate the position in which you plant a herb; for instance, if you put pineapple mint at the side of a path, some of the shoots will overgrow the path, and are bound to be trodden on, so that an elusive scent of pineapple and mint follows in the wake of the passerby.

CULINARY HERBS

Mint
The mints are an amazing group of plants for variety of aroma; the leaves of pepper mint are the actual source of that aroma and flavour, though neither tastes or smells in the slightest way like the pepper used for savoury foods.

There are two pepper mints, the white form called *Mentha × piperita officinalis*, which has light green leaves, and black pepper mint, *M. × piperita piperita*, whose leaves and stems have a dark, almost black flush to them. It looks very handsome planted where it can grow through a white flowering saxifrage, or the grey-leaved and white-flowered snow-in-summer (*Cerastium tomentosum*), and does not seem to get out of hand in these positions. Both these groundcover plants are as strong-growing as the mint, and they keep one another in check, though snow-in-summer still needs shearing back occasionally to stop it insinuating itself amongst its neighbours. Height of either mint is about 45–60 cm (18–24 in), and the tiny lilac flowers appear in mid to late summer in clusters at the top of the stems.

In complete contrast is the soft aroma of apple mint, whose rounded woolly leaves exactly mimic the fruit in their odour. It is an even taller and more vigorous mint, which needs care with its planting so that it doesn't take over a whole bed. Its leaves are plain green, so put it beside a path, to be brushed against, along with pineapple mint, whose white-edged leaves are much more decorative and eye-catching, and enjoy the contrast in perfumes.

Ginger mint (*M. × gentilis*) is best grown in the form of 'Variegata', which has bright yellow-striped, shiny, pointed leaves on dark purple stems, with lilac flowers in mid summer; its alternative name of orange mint depends on its owner's nose. Watch for the fungus disease rust on it, which it tends to succumb to, though pineapple mint growing next to it will be immune.

A mint with a genuine perfume is 'Eau de Cologne' mint (*M. × piperita citrata*), a dark-flushed kind rather like black pepper mint, but with rounded leaves, not pointed ones. It will smell best and be darker coloured in a sunny place. Oddly enough it is thought to have the same parents as pepper mint but has somehow managed to produce a completely different smell.

None of these mints is difficult to grow; planted in a mixed border or island bed, you are likely to be chopping out large pieces of the crown and creeping rhizomes every year, as they try to infiltrate flowering perennial neighbours. They need a strict eye kept on them through the growing season, and in spring you will be surprised to see how far away from the parent clump new shoots are appearing, sneaking up amongst the stems of shrubs and through clumps of bulbs.

Rosemary

There is a group of commonly used culinary herbs whose aromas, though sharp and penetrating, are enjoyable, and whose leaves are of enormous value in adding to the flavour of food. One of them is rosemary (*Rosmarinus officinalis*), not only one of the best herbs to use in cooking, but also an outstanding garden plant.

The narrow greyish green leaves are evergreen, clothing branches up to 1.5 m (5 ft) tall, more if it likes the soil and situation. If a leaf or two is crushed and the pungent aroma inhaled, it will trickle up the nostrils into the cavities behind the forehead, clearing and refreshing as it goes, in much the same way as eucalyptus or menthol, but with a less medicinal air—it is almost a perfume.

In spring it bursts into a mass of small light blue flowers, which the bees adore, lasting several weeks. Sometimes, flowering starts in late winter and goes on for several months, and in some seasons flowering is repeated in late summer. If you want a change from the standard rosemary, there is a white-flowered form, 'Alba'; a vertical one called 'Miss Jessup's Upright', hardier than other varieties; the pink-flowered 'Majorcan Pink', and 'Fota Blue', whose flowers are a much more vivid blue.

Rosemary grows best in a hot sunny place, and poor but well-drained, chalky soil. Once established it will survive all but the severest cold, and the common kind spreads a good 1.2–1.5 m (4–5 ft) wide. It fits in well to a mixed border of grey-leaved plants, and would make a good centre to a herb garden. Paving sets off its grey foliage and rather formal habit, so it would also fit well on a terrace or patio, or in a space in the paving. Container growing suits it, too, and one of the Georgian style or Provencal terracotta pots or tubs planted with rosemary would make an eye-catching feature. It roots easily from summer heel cuttings.

Thyme

The savories and thymes are particularly strong-smelling herbs, both with small leaves, but with what a concentration of aroma! Garden thyme (*Thymus vulgaris*) is a tough little bush about 23 cm (9 in) tall and as much wide, evergreen except in severe winters, which will kill it in any case; and lemon thyme (*T. × citriodorus*) is similar, but has slightly larger leaves having a strong lemon fragrance; in great heat the aroma of both species will fill the air.

The leaves of both species are plain green, but there is a pretty variety called

'Silver Posie' with light grey leaves edged with white, adding to its aromatic charms. Always give this one sun, shelter and good drainage as it is not as hardy as the others. Another thyme called 'Doone Valley' is low-growing, a halfway house between a creeping thyme, and the bushy types. At first glance it is not obviously a thyme, as its dark green leaves are bright yellow at the tips of the shoots. It looks most attractive, and still has the characteristic aroma of thyme.

All these thymes have masses of tiny flowers in varying intensities of pink-purple, in early and mid summer, lasting for several weeks. In mild seasons flowering will start in mid spring and last even longer and, like rosemary, the thymes are always alive with bees.

Savory

The savories, summer and winter (*Satureja hortensis* and *S. montana*) are equally bee-attractive, particularly the winter white-flowered one. This is hardy and perennial, a small shrub, growing to about 23 cm (9 in) high and nearly as wide, unlike summer savory, which is an annual, growing taller to 30 cm (12 in) and with a purple flush to leaves and stems, and tiny lilac or pink flowers from mid summer. The small leaves are especially pungent smelling, and are almost as strong as pepper or a spice—traditionally, savory leaves are used with beans to bring out their flavour.

Neither is difficult to grow, but if you are starting with seed, sow winter savory in late summer and do not cover it with soil, otherwise it does not germinate. Summer savory can be sown outdoors in mid–late spring in the usual way. Winter savory is a good little container plant for a trough just outside the kitchen door, and only needs shearing back after flowering to cut off the flowered stems. Summer savory is even more decorative and worth a place in the garden borders. Chalky soil and sun are the ideal growing conditions.

Lovage

Though parsley has a strong flavour, it is not really aromatic, and does not merit inclusion here, but lovage (*Ligusticum officinalis*) does. Rub one of the lobes of its large leaves and you will be almost overpowered by the yeasty celery aroma; in fact, you can detect the plant from a distance as the stems and flowers are also aromatic and invade the surrounding air accordingly. Tall and handsome, the hollow flowering stems end in yellow-flowered umbels in mid and late summer, towering 2.1 m (7 ft) above the ground. It is definitely a plant for the back of the border, not minding shade, and needing plenty of permanent space and a strong, deep, moist soil.

Sage

In complete contrast, the evergreen sages are low-growing, 45–60 cm (18–24 in) tall, small bushy shrubs, with powerfully aromatic leaves and a somewhat bitter flavour. Sage is a good medicinal, as well as culinary, herb in the form *Salvia officinalis*, and sage tea was once universally drunk, as Indian tea is nowadays. This form does not flower in Britain, though it will do so in warmer climates; for regular flowering grow *S. angustifolia*, whose narrow grey-green leaves provide a foil for the spikes of blue-violet flowers in late spring and early summer, to which bees will home in.

Besides the narrow-leaved sage, there are three others whose aromatic leaves are not just plain green but prettily coloured: 'Icterina' with yellow-edged, light green foliage; 'Tricolor', leaves edged creamy white and tinted purple, and 'Pur-

Rosemary is a shrubby herb whose decorativeness alone justifies its place in the garden; its aromatic leaves are a delightful added bonus.

The coloured leaved aromatic sages make a pretty group; shown here are Salvia *'Icterina', yellow leaved, S.* angustifolia, *narrow-leaved, and S. 'Purpurascens', purple leaved.*

purascens', which has an overall deep purple tone to the leaves. All like sun, shelter and good drainage and, if flowering stems do appear, they need to be removed, otherwise the plants lose their compact habit. 'Tricolor' is the least hardy and needs protection from frost; 'Purpurascens' turns an even deeper purple in cold weather, but will survive short-lived moderate frosts. Planted together in clumps, they make a pretty patchwork of colours the year round; the purple-toned ones would fit well into a grey or silver border to contrast the lighter foliage, and have the further advantage that they like the same conditions of growth.

Elder

The elder (*Sambucus nigra*), whose rankly aromatic leaves are not very pleasant to inhale, is a quick-growing bushy hedgerow tree found throughout Europe, having a tendency to become gaunt in appearance. Although the berries and flowers justify it a place in this chapter, the green-leaved species is rather plain, and the variety 'Aurea' is much to be preferred. Even better is 'Aurea Laciniata' whose leaves are much cut and deeply serrated as well as being yellow. When clusters of small white flowers appear in mid summer, you will have a delicate fragrance as well, which can be retained in sparkling wine made from them; the deep red-black berries which follow them in autumn supply a full-bodied red wine redolent of the same aroma.

Sweet bay, dill and fennel

Like parsley, sweet bay (*Laurus nobilis*) is a culinary herb whose aromatic merit is not great, though its flavour is strong, one of the strongest of the cooking herbs. Even in hot sun it does not exude an aroma. Neither do dill and fennel, again, leafy herbs full of flavour. Rubbing their feathery leaves between the fingers does release an aroma, a pleasantly sweetish one, almost aniseed-like. Dill (*Anethum graveolens*) is an annual; fennel (*Foeniculum vulgare*) is a perennial. Never grow them as neighbours as the resultant seedlings will be neither one nor the other. Dill grows 60 cm (2 ft) tall and has tiny yellow flowers in umbels in mid summer; fennel is a large plant 1.5 m (5 ft) tall, handsome with its filmy thread-like foliage forming a cloud round the polished stems. For even more decoration as well as aroma, grow the bronze fennel, *F. vulgare purpureum*, with brown tinged stems and leaves for about half the growing season, especially when young.

Marjoram

All three of the marjorams are pungent, but the best aroma comes from sweet marjoram, a tender annual which prefers warm sunny weather, and in cool climates needs the protection of glass to grow really well. Wild marjoram—the oregano of Spain and Italy—and pot marjoram are 'rubbing' herbs, strong-smelling and hot flavoured, too hot to sample raw but perfect for cooking. Their dark green leaves are about 2.5 cm (1 in) long, and the tiny pink-purple or white flowers appear in clusters late in the summer on 30-cm (12-in) stems in the case of *Origanum onites* (pot marjoram), 45–75-cm (1¹/₂–2¹/₂-ft) stems for *O. vulgare* (the wild form).

The oregano of the Mediterranean hillsides has a much better aroma than that found in Britain, with a smoky overtone which adds the authentic flavour to pizzas and spaghetti sauces. If seeds or a plant from the Continent can be obtained, the leaves from the subsequent plants will keep this flavour in cooler climates, which suggests that it is a true variety, distinct from the British wild marjoram.

Neither of these is particularly ornamental, though the bees like the flowers, and they do provide colour at a time when flowers can be rather few and far between. However, there is a golden marjoram, (*O. vulgare aureum*), a low-growing mound of small yellow leaves which gradually elongates as the leafy flowering shoots develop, to be topped in late summer with pinkish flowers. Kept short, it will finish off the edge of a bed or border; specimen clumps dispersed through a rock border or rock garden provide patches of bright colour, or can be used in a golden bed, with golden thyme (*Thymus vulgaris*), the yellow-leaved sage 'Icterina', the yellow-variegated lemon balm (*Melissa officinalis*) and the yellow-leaved form of feverfew (*Tanacetum partheniumaureum*).

Lemon balm

I mentioned earlier a lemon-flavoured form of thyme; balm (*Melissa officinalis*) is another herb with a strong lemon scent and flower, an undistinguished herb in appearance growing into a bushy many-stemmed plant nearly 90 cm (3 ft) tall, clothed in soft, heart-shaped leaves with toothed edges. The variegated variety is eye-catching, with splashes of vivid yellow on the leaves from spring until half-way through the summer. Then its flowering stems shoot up and it becomes faded and speckly—it is best kept cut low and not allowed to flower.

Like other herbs which are unassuming in appearance, lemon balm well repays leaf-rubbing. A garden which is planted irregularly with these 'rubbing' herbs makes a delightful one to wander through, on a scented trail, each stopping point marked by a different aroma as you sample a leaf from the thymes, another from apple mint, a third from lovage, and yet another from one which is perhaps my favourite of them all, balm of Gilead—surprisingly little known in view of its astonishing aroma and ease of cultivation.

HOUSEHOLD HERBS

Balm of Gilead

Cedronella triphylla, or balm of Gilead is one of several herbal plants with this common name, another being *Commiphora opobalsamum*, and it is this one which is mentioned in the Bible. In those days it only grew in the area known as Yemen, and was later introduced into Palestine and other Middle Eastern countries, where great value was put on the aromatic gum obtained from the bark and fruit. It is a small evergreen tree with three-parted leaves and white flowers, also in threes. Another species of the same genus, *C. myrrha*, provides myrrh and, like balm of Gilead, is a native of the Yemen and surrounding area; neither can be grown in cool–temperate climates.

However, *Cedronella triphylla*, from the Canary Islands, does well outdoors in the warmth of temperate summers, when it will grow at least 60 cm (2 ft) tall. In its native Canaries it is nearer 1.2 m (4 ft) and correspondingly wide, with pointed leaflets in threes, and short, muddy-purple spikes of tiny white or very pale purple flowers in mid and late summer. It will die down in autumn, and be killed by frost, but the seeds will self-sow, liking to establish between paving slabs in a sunny place, and you should never be without it, once obtained.

The pungency of its aroma is outstanding, as is the variety of scents contained in it, a mixture of lemon, menthol, camphor and spices, strong enough to kill any germ at six paces by its smell alone. This one is a 'must' for the side of a path, or anywhere that it is likely to be bruised by the passerby. Plant a good flowering perennial next to it to make up for its plain appearance, such as campanulas or day lilies (hemerocallis), or another herb like the brillantly blue-flowered, starry borage which never stops flowering.

Balm of Gilead is not a cooking herb, but it does add a lovely spicy kick to a mixture of household herbs which might otherwise smell too bitter to be pleasant, and therefore unacceptable to us. Sometimes in warm weather you can catch a whiff of it in the air, but it and the majority of this group of herbs is another whose plants are 'fast . . . of their smells', to quote Francis Bacon again. Their characteristic smell is one which encourages sneezing and they were once used on floors, in bed linen and amongst clothes to ward off a variety of insects intent on sharing one's home. With the advent of central heating and fitted carpets in many modern houses, they seem likely to be of use again, if only to discourage the parasites on cats and dogs.

Nevertheless, nearly all of these are garden plants now grown for their appearance; many were also once used medicinally. Some were the standard equivalents of modern insecticides but safe to use, scattered about indoors in the home and other buildings—churches, the law courts and the Royal Court itself. In fact, there was an official Royal post of 'Strewer of Herbs in Ordinary to His Majesty', still in evidence for George IV's coronation.

Sweet Cicely

Sweet Cicely (*Myrrhis odorata*) provides the link between culinary and household aromatic herbs, as its strong aniseed scent is also its flavour. The large lobed leaves are often mistaken for those of another umbellifer, cow parsley (*Anthriscus sylvestris*) and so are the clusters of tiny white flowers, but the aroma is unmistakable, and present in stems and roots as well as leaves. This sweetish odour can be used to take the place of some of the sugar used to sweeten cooked fruit, but if too many leaves are used the aniseed flavour overwhelms that of the fruit.

Sweet Cicely will grow in sun or shade—woodland areas suit its habit well—and a moist, deep soil which needs to be acid or neutral. Make your choice of site carefully, as its roots are large, fleshy, numerous and tenacious, altogether much like an octopus and, once established, the plant is a brute to get out again. The roots were once eaten like an ordinary root vegetable. It will self-sow lavishly, but the seeds need to be frosted before they will germinate, and may take up to eighteen months to do so.

Curry plant

Grey and silver borders can easily consist only of plants which need sun and good soil drainage and, given the hot sun they need, will produce a heavily aromatic smell pervading much of the garden on a summer day. A blend of the aromas of thyme, sage summer savory and rosemary can be spiced with that of the curry plant, another purely silver plant with narrow leaves only about 2 mm (¹/₈ in) wide, all the way up 45-cm (18-in) stems. In warmth they give off a strong hot smell of curry, as they do if rubbed, but curiously have no flavour, and are not used in cooking. The curry plant (*Helichrysum angustifolium*) has clusters of small round yellow flower-heads, if allowed to, but it really is a better plant if flowering is prevented—it gets very stalky otherwise.

Sweet flag

In mediaeval times the only floor coverings would be animal skins and certain types of plants put straight down on to beaten soil or stone. Rushes in the form of *Acorus calamus* were one of the favourites for strewing like this; they lasted well and smelled sweetly and strongly of cinnamon when bruised. The sweet flag is a plant for watersides, where it grows happily in boggy soil. Height is at least 90 cm (3 ft) and if you get the variegated form whose leaves are lined with yellow and creamy white, you will have one of the most ornamental plants for water gardening, especially when its greenish-yellow spikes of flowers appear in mid summer.

Both the leaves and the roots are aromatic and, when dried, and crumbled, are an essential ingredient for making up household herb mixtures. The ancient Greeks used the powder from the roots in their beds and clothing, and Thomas à Becket ordered his hall to be strewed with freshly gathered sweet rushes so that 'such knights as the benches could not contain, might sit on the floor without dirtying their clothes.'

Rue

Another household herb, very popular in mediaeval days, is rue (*Ruta graveolens*), a small shrub with filigree-like leaves, 'divided into wings', to quote Gerard, and clusters of mustard-yellow flowers in early and mid summer. The pretty delicate leaves alone warrant it a place in the ornamental garden, but the blue-leaved form of the species 'Jackman's Blue' doubles its attraction, while retaining the typical aroma. It grows wild on the Mediterranean hillsides where it often looks rather scruffy, but give it a moderate and well-drained soil with

The curry plant, Helichrysum angustifolium, *is a silver leaved plant producing a strong smell of curry, though it does not have that flavour and is therefore not used in cooking.*

plenty of sun, and it will cover itself in foliage. It well repays clipping back to keep it rounded and small, and a row of these blue balls in square stone containers along the edge of a sunny terrace or patio would make an arresting feature.

Rue must be one of the most bitter-smelling of plants; to quote Gerard again: 'this Rue hath a very strong and ranke smell, and a biting taste'.

Hyssop

Another favourite household and medicinal herb of mediaeval and Elizabethan times is hyssop, *Hyssopus officinalis*, which has the same provenance as rue, and is similarly a low-growing shrub, nearly evergreen in cool–temperate climates. It has a delightful aroma, quite strong and sweet, with a faint overtone of lemon and spiciness blending to produce its own characteristic smell. When distilled, the essential oil is a popular base for perfumes, and also, oddly enough, it is used in making Chartreuse liqueur. Hyssop's unique aroma will blend with the honey produced by the bees from its flowers, which they visit in their hundreds, to produce an outstandingly good conserve in the same class as thyme or heather honey.

As a garden plant, hyssop is an ornamental little plant, flowering in mid and late summer, usually with spike-like clusters of deep purple blue-violet flowers, though there are varieties with pink or white flowers as well. It needs to be clipped after flowering otherwise it gets straggly and, while it likes sun and good drainage, the soil should not be too starved, since it again becomes weak and lanky.

The contrast between the aromas of these household and all the other herbs is fascinating; it is difficult to believe that there could be so many different smells amongst a single group of plants, especially as it is the leaves that contain them, rather than the flowers. Sniffing them one after another induces a pleasant kind of nasal surfeit which often finishes up in an enjoyable convulsion of sneezing. Two more which are liable to bring this on rather quickly are lavender cotton (*Santolina chamecyparissus*) and southernwood or lad's love (*Artemisia abrotanum*).

Lavender cotton

Lavender cotton is a silvery grey-leaved plant, a good decorative evergrey whose stems and tiny leaves are clothed with wool. From southern Europe, its height is usually about 30–38 cm (12–15 in), though it can be 50 cm (20 in) high, and as much wide; in mid–late summer clusters of ball-like, bright yellow flowers are produced. With flowering it gets leggy, and the stems should be clipped back before they elongate; a gentle back and sides in mid spring will also keep it dense and compact.

One of the reasons for its popularity with mediaeval gardeners was that it could be sheared in this way without harm, and so it would make a good edging hedge for the beds of their formal gardens. Another was its potential as a moth repellent; it has an aroma verging on the bitter, like rue.

Southernwood

Southernwood (*Artemisia abrotanum*) is a filmy-leaved sub-shrub; it was described by the first-century Greek army doctor Dioscorides as 'having very small leaves as if it were seen rather as if furnished with hair'. The light grey-green foliage gives the upright shoots an ethereal appearance; they grow quickly each summer to about 90 cm (3 ft) tall. It does not like cold, and the top growth will be killed by moderate frost, but the crown should shoot again. In any case, if the stems are not cut back by cold, they must certainly be cut back hard to prevent legginess at the base, in mid spring. Its aroma is strong, bitter and slightly lemony; it was once used to repel flies and moths by hanging bunches up in kitchens and *garderobes* or wardrobes.

Absinthe

One of southernwood's relatives, *Artemisia absinthium*, also called wormwood, is one of the most bitter herbs there is, being an ingredient of absinthe, as well as vermouth, another 'dry'-flavoured drink. It bears garden cultivation, and should be grown more than it is, being a handsome, grey-leaved sub-shrub growing to 90 cm (3 ft) tall and about 60 cm (2 ft) wide. You can see it growing beside fields and on waste places throughout Europe, so it is not difficult to grow. The variety 'Lambrook Silver' is a less tall, silvery leaved version, still aromatic, and even more desirable. Both artemisias are easily grown in most soils and some sun.

Feverfew

You could fill a grey/silver border with the aromatic herbs described; a golden border is a good companion, or it can be used to lighten a patch where there is shade at some time during the day. For this, golden feverfew is one of the most dazzling and longlasting. Common feverfew has plain green feathery leaves about 7 cm (3 in) long, and single white daisy flowers in clusters in early–mid summer; *Tanacetum parthenium aureum* has intensely yellow leaves in a mound about 15 cm (6 in) high and as much across, until its 23–30-cm (9–12-in)

*The leaves of feverfew (*Tanacetum parthenium*) are bitterly aromatic, and its golden-leaved form is not only decorative but also easily grown.*

flower-stems appear in mid summer, nearly a foot shorter than its relative.

Both the species and the variety are strongly aromatic, bitter to taste and to smell, and one of the few herbs the bees will not go near. All the same, it self-seeds with gay abandon, and you will find tiny yellow seedlings of *aureum* in particular coming up everywhere, if you let it flower. It is a short-lived perennial, remaining leafy through the winter, though the yellow one will succumb to intense cold.

Alecost

An unusual relative of feverfew is alecost, or the camphor plant, *Chrysanthemum balsamita*, now called *Balsamita major*. It is one of these plants which confuses the botanist, as it was also once called *Tanacetum balsamita*, and it has an alternative common name, too, costmary, from the Latin *costus*, meaning an Oriental plant, and Mary, the name of Our Lady with whom the plant was much associated in mediaeval days.

I love the grey-green, almost mealy leaves of this herb, with their finely toothed edges, and their refreshing aromatic mixture of balsam and camphor. More than any of the others, this seems to be a good plant for repelling moths and flies, and is one of the best for adding to pot pourris; used as a bookmark, a dried leaf will invest the pages permanently with its fragrance. It was once used for clearing and flavouring beer, until hops took its place. It is perennial, growing 90–120 cm (3–4 ft) tall, and spreading at ground level about 45 cm (18 in) wide. The small yellow, button-like flowers appear in late summer and autumn, but are not particularly decorative. A native of western Asia, it grows easily in any soil but water-logged ones, and in sun or some shade.

Tansy

Tansy is called *Tanacetum vulgare*, another in the daisy family with yellow balls of flowers in sprays during mid and late summer. The dark green, frondy leaves are definitely bitterly aromatic—there is no sweetness about these—but had a place in Elizabethan cookery, in tansy puddings and tansy cakes. It is also one of the older insecticides, the pungent leaves being used for strewing, and for keeping meat free of flies. It hates badly drained soil, and will die in it, but give it a light well drained one and sun or shade, and it will flourish and spread with alacrity by tough, creeping, underground stems, growing as much as 120 cm (4 ft) tall above ground.

Catnep

So far, the household herbs described have been ornamental, but one of the most interesting, as far as aromas are concerned, is one which looks and grows like a weed. This is the genuine catnep, *Nepeta cataria*, not the garden one *N. faasenii*, which has beauty but no soul. *N. cataria* looks much like a nettle in leaf and habit; the tiny flowers are white, in mid–late summer, in clusters forming a kind of spike, and it grows about 90 cm (3 ft) tall in clumps 45 cm (18 in) wide.

The aroma is pungent and not particularly pleasant, but the effect it has on cats has to be seen to be believed. They will roll on it and tear it to pieces with their claws; bags of the dried and crumbled leaves get wiped across their foreheads and licked madly, and general chaos ensues for about five minutes. Rats are said to dislike it intensely, so it would be useful grown close to chicken or duck houses, and it has some medicinal use still. As a perennial plant, native to Britain and Europe, it is easily grown in cool–temperate climates, and seed sown outdoors in spring germinates without trouble.

Lavender

The most long-used and loved household herb of all is lavender, *Lavandula angustifolia* (syn. *L. officinalis*), an evergrey shrub, growing about 75 cm (2½ ft) tall, and sprawling more widely. The perfume of its flowers is delightful, and although there are lavender varieties with deeper blue-violet flowers, and pink or white ones, the lack of perfume in these so-called improvements destroys the whole essence of the plant—without its perfume surely it is not lavender?

It was certainly grown in Britain during the twelfth century, and was probably a Roman introduction; the Romans and Greeks used its oil extensively to add to bathing and laundering water, and to perfume the skin, though the Greeks had more medicinal uses for it. The lavender used for this is likely to have been *L. stoechas*, or French lavender, susceptible to frost but intensely perfumed, with deep purple flowers and silvery hairy stems. From ancient times the lavender flower has been used in some form for the sake of its perfume; it has been a strewing herb, an essential ingredient, as it still is, of pot pourris, the only constituent of muslin bags for linen and wardrobes, and a perfume for gloves and leather.

Sun and well drained calcareous soil are important to its well-being, and to the strength of its fragrance, but it also needs some plant nutrient, so give it an annual dressing of rotted organic matter in spring. Heavy snow will make a bush into an ungainly sprawl, and tying it together beforehand helps to prevent this; shearing it over before new growth starts in spring will also keep it dense and encourage new shoots to appear from low down, early in its life. *L. stoechas* will not grow in chalky soil.

Gather the flower spikes just after the flowers have opened completely, in the cool of early morning, and hang them to dry in a dark warm place. Even the stalks are fragrant, and if burnt will scent the surrounding air.

DESIGNING WITH HERBS

Because lavender will stand clipping like this, it and its dwarf variant were used as edgings to the intricate knot gardens so popular from the beginning of the sixteenth century until well into the eighteenth century. Santolina, rosemary, thyme and hyssop were others used in the same way, as they still could be in our own herb gardens and knot gardens, giving the garden air a glorious mixture of aromas and perfumes on a hot day.

A herb garden could be designed in the form of a simple knot; provided the beds are symmetrical, the design can be entirely your own. Originally it consisted of continuous interlacing bands, thus representing infinity, and the sign for infinity could in fact be used, perhaps one at right angles to the other within a diamond whose sides are curved. Paths would outline the shapes, and plants would fill these in; the centre might be a specimen plant such as clipped bay, or a sundial, an old-fashioned beehive, or an arbour containing a seat.

If you do not have the room for an entire herb garden, a herb border is a worthwhile substitute, especially if it faces the sun. As so many aromatic herbs are evergreen, it will look good all year round, and the variations in foliage colouring will give it a more than usually three-dimensional appearance, with the bonus of flowers from many of them in summer. Heights are varied as well, so that altogether, with the backing of an evergreen hedge such as yew or holly, it could easily be as decorative as a conventional herbaceous border.

If you would nevertheless rather give your border over to herbaceous perennials, but would like some herbal aromas in the garden, they fit easily into random plantings where the surroundings suit their needs. The curry plant, *Artemisia* 'Lambrook Silver' and rosemary will all be at home in sun and dry soils; shade and moist soil are no problem to lemon balm and catmint; the thymes are ideal for rock gardens, and a foliage rock border would supply homes for the sages, winter savory and variegated lemon balm. Rosemary and rue would be pretty in containers on paving, and creeping thymes are perfect for the paving itself. By doing this you can have your cake and eat it; you can easily fit in fifty different herbs and yet still have room, in a small garden, for the other types of plants—shrubs and perennials, bulbs, annuals and roses, vegetables and fruit—which are, naturally, all scented or aromatic!

Lavender's scent is one of the most familiar and popular, and its use can be traced back to classical times.

CHAPTER EIGHT

SCENTED LAWNS AND GROUNDCOVERS

Before the time of the mechanical mower there was no such thing as an area of short smooth grass in gardens. Any ground covered in grass was nearly always part of a large estate, and was measured in acres, which were kept cut by scythes to a height of several centimetres. Gardens were always composed of flower beds (parterres), paths, gravelled areas, kitchen gardens and orchards, in which there was even longer grass mixed with wild flowers.

When an implement for cutting grass to 1.5 cm ($^1/_2$ in) arrived on the gardening scene, garden owners everywhere realized overnight that such an area of grass could be kept shaved, with a minimum of labour, and all the business of digging, weeding, raking, dividing, tying up and deadheading that went with beds and borders could be avoided. Besides, an outdoor carpet of this kind was undoubtedly a superb foil for the other plants, and it provided a space on which one could sit, play games—croquet was one of them—hold social gatherings and leave the children to play in safety.

However, there is more to a lawn's care than mowing it once a week; moreover, an unshaven lawn does nothing for the garden's appearance and if left, it gets to the point when a machine other than a mower is needed to deal with it. A conventional lawn is undoubtedly a tie, and involves a good deal of work.

HERBAL LAWNS

There are alternatives to grass which need very little work, and which are scented or aromatic. Some of them are suitable for walking or sitting on, some are simply labour-saving; however, although they will prevent the plants that you do not want from growing, they cannot be used in the same way as a lawn.

Thyme
One of the best and most aromatic alternatives to grass is the creeping version of thyme; it naturally grows flat against the ground and so is not affected by traffic over it, nor does it need to be mown. The stems of *Thymus serpyllum* lie on the ground and grow along the soil surface, rooting into it from the leaf-joints. Its tiny, dark green leaves are highly aromatic, and one's footsteps are followed by a trail of scented air, the more powerful when they are wet after rain.

Creeping thyme is a native of most European countries, flourishing best in the warmer ones, where it will be found growing on stony or rocky ground, sandy soils and anywhere, including slopes or hillsides, where the terrain is well-drained. It hybridizes with ease, with the help of pollinating insects, particularly bees, and will self-seed, gradually forming a dense mat of mixed shades of pink, pink-purple, lilac and purple.

Another mat-forming tough little thyme is the caraway-scented one, *T. herba-barona*, whose pale pink flowers are produced in rounded heads. It grows wild in Corsica and Sardinia, and its specific name is a reference to the fact that sprigs of it used to be rubbed on a baron of beef before roasting. As well as the aromas of thyme and caraway, you could add the nose-tingling smell of pine by mixing *T. caespititius* with the planting. This has light green, narrower leaves than the other two but, like them, the lilac-pink flowers are a magnet for bees.

Altogether these thymes will form a patchwork of colour—in summer a mixture of pinks and purples, in winter a blend of shades of green. None is difficult to grow, given a well-drained soil and a sunny place, and they can form the centre of a herb garden, cover a bank, thus doing away with the difficulty of mowing a grassy slope, or carpet the ground of an arbour. They will not take the place of grass on a full-size lawn, but are more than adequate for small areas that are inconvenient to mow.

Pennyroyal

A sunny, well-drained site is liable to be difficult to grow good grass on in any case, as it will be hot and dry in summer; grass needs reserves of moisture in the soil. However, the size and shape of a site also dictates the choice of plant to grow there and, even if the soil is suitably moist, the shape or slope can make the site awkward to mow. For a moist area pennyroyal would make a good grass substitute, as it needs water. It is one of the mints, *Mentha pulegium*, and one of the oldest in cultivation, being much used both medicinally and in cooking. The aroma is strong, in fact the strongest of all the mints, and although the Elizabethans used it in their food, it has since gradually disappeared from the flavouring herbs list.

It grows wild throughout Europe and Asia, growing close to streams and pools, and rapidly forming mats of small dark green leaves about 1.5 cm ($^1/_2$ in) long on stems which root at the leaf-joints. The tiny pink-purple flowers appear in whorls up the stems in mid and late summer, but the few flowering stems that are produced tend to lie on the soil surface as well in the variety *M. decumbens*, which is the most suitable one for a grass substitute. The other, *M. p. erecta*, can grow a foot tall, and is much more floriferous and much less mat-forming.

The name has an interesting history in that it is derived from *puliol royale*, the French word for thyme, the plant being considered the best of the varieties; in Britain it was called *piliole-rial* by the mediaeval botanists. The specific name *pulegium* came from the Latin *pulex*, a flea, since its ability to ward off these insects was thought to be considerable.

It germinates easily from seed sown in late spring, provided it has protection, but the more usual way to start it off is by division of plants or runners, spacing them 15 cm (6 in) apart each way in early autumn or mid–late spring; supply water if the weather is at all dry after planting. A light mowing or shearing twice in the growing season is all that is necessary to keep it tidy. After about five years it will begin to be thin in patches so it is a good idea to take runners in autumn and grow on in a nursery bed for filling in gaps, especially as moderate to severe frosts can kill it.

Corsican Mint

The Corsican mint, *Mentha requienii*, lends itself as an aromatic substitute for grass, provided it does not have a great deal of traffic over it, and provided the site is sheltered, warm and well-drained—cold will see it off. Its round, light green leaves are really tiny, only about 2 mm (¹/₈ in) wide, but form a dense mat on creeping, rooting stems, and equally small lilac flowers appear in mid summer. The aroma is strongly pepperminty, and it needs no mowing. Plant about 7–10 cm (3–4 in) apart.

Chamomile

All the aromatic plants mentioned so far have been herbs, and the plant that is best known as a grass substitute is also a herb, chamomile (*Chamaemelum nobile*), whose strong apple-like fragrance accounts for its name. The Greek word *melon* means apple, and *kamai* is 'on the ground', and there is still a type of sherry made, called manzanilla, meaning little apple, which is flavoured with chamomile. As well as its considerable medicinal and garden value, chamomile was much used as a household herb for floors because of its fragrance, and is still worth using nowadays in moth repellent mixtures.

As with aromatic plants in general, this fragrance is most noticeable after rain, but the traffic of feet or machinery over it also releases a powerful aroma and, as this treatment only seems to encourage its growth and spread, it is ideal for small lawns. There are two types, one which has white daisy flowers, and one which is flowerless, the 'Treneague' variety, and it is the latter that is most suitable for lawns—it has a much more mat-like habit of growth and requires little cutting.

Chamomile has light green feathery leaves on low-growing stems, which remain green even in dry weather. To do well it needs sandyish or other well-drained soil, and sun; shade does not suit it. If planted in mid spring about 10 cm (4 in) apart, it will have made a good cover by mid summer, provided it has been kept weeded. It will need shearing over, or mowing lightly, two or three times a year; if it becomes thin here and there, a topdressing mixture of peat and sand will encourage it to root and thicken up.

In a herb garden chamomile is ideal as a central lawn, or to cover the paths; it could also be used in a chess-board pattern between other herbs, and would make a good 'rug' in front of a garden seat, instead of paving.

Yarrow

There is no reason why yarrow (*Achillea millefolium*) should not be used as a grass substitute. After all, it often grows so well on grass lawns that one might as well abandon the grass and let the yarrow take over. With constant mowing, it becomes very flat, and its dark green ferny leaves cover the soil well on stems which are tough, low-growing and intricately woven. Its foliage has a strong and not unpleasantly bitter aroma, and it would be perfect if it did not die down almost completely in winter, though in mild gardens it is likely to retain most of its leaves.

It is another old medicinal herb, still used by medical herbalists, and was also once an ingredient of snuff; not for nothing is one of its relations, *A. ptarmica*, called sneezewort, and yarrow tea is said to be a good cure for colds. Planted about 15 cm (6 in) apart in spring, its creeping and rooting stems will soon cover the ground. It grows easily from seed as well as from divisions and, because of this, flowering should be severely discouraged, as it will be if kept mown. Otherwise you are likely to have yarrow lawns on the flowerbeds, from which it will be exceedingly difficult to eliminate.

Choice of site is also important, so that you can confine it easily and keep it strictly within the area where it is meant to grow. Close to paving is not ideal, as it can easily slip underneath and then appear between the cracks, and removal would entail lifting the paving to ensure its complete eradication. Sun or a little shade is suitable, and so are the majority of soils.

All these plants are good as substitutes for grass to make little lawns, and to provide a green patch in odd corners, to be used as centres in formal garden designs, and so on. All are capable of forming a flat, close carpet of green—a cover for the ground—and all of them are herbs.

GROUNDCOVERS

There is, however, another group of aromatic plants, ground-covering plants which are low-growing, but which are not by any means substitutes for grass. They are much too tall, cannot be mown or sheared, and are mostly grown for their fragrant flowers rather than their foliage. The scope for using these in the garden is much greater since they can be an essential part of the design and placing of beds, trees, shrubs and water.

Sweet woodruff

Sweet woodruff (*Asperula odorata*) which serves to introduce this group is primarily a green groundcover, an unremarkable small plant with whorls of light green leaves on stems about 23 cm (9 in) tall, on top of which there are clusters of small, star-like, white flowers in early summer. It is perennial and creeps about underground, sending up stems from the rootstock so that it effectively covers the ground in the area in which it is planted. None of it is aromatic while it is growing, but as it dies down and dries in late summer and early autumn, it develops a strong and delightful smell of newly mown grass. Because of this it was another herb used for refreshing the house; bunches of the dried stems were hung in the rooms in the heat of summer which, according to Gerard, did 'very well attemper the air, cool and make fresh the place'.

Unlike many aromatic herbs, sweet woodruff actually needs to grow in shade, being found naturally growing in the lee of hedges and in woods, so it is a pretty and effective groundcover for areas under specimen trees, where it is difficult to grow grass, and under the kind of shrubs whose branches do not reach to the soil, but where it is difficult to mow.

It does a good job under roses, too, even though it disappears in winter, and it will fit into a good many corners that other groundcovers will take exception to, but it does need moisture, and well-drained or 'hot' soils are no good to it. Spacing is about 30 cm (1 ft), and planting is in spring; it can be divided after flowering as well, in mid summer—any plantings then will need good watering.

Lily-of-the-valley

Another flowering plant which likes a little shade and is a native of European woodlands is lily-of-the-valley, *Convallaria majalis*, a true lily surprisingly, in view of its small flowers. Like woodruff, it is white-flowered, with a one-sided row of tiny, toothed bells hanging from flowering stems about 20 cm (8 in) tall, in the late spring and early summer. Their fragrance is proverbial, permeating the air around them, and many perfumes contain its fragrance as one of the main ingredients.

One of the most difficult areas in a garden to plant up is dry shade, but lily-of-the-valley is tailor-made for such areas, as it is found growing in woodlands where the soil is well-drained, or dry because of the tree cover. Although it dies down in winter, each shoot produces two oval pointed leaves in early spring and, because it has creeping fleshy underground stems, it can spread rapidly and cover the soil by sending up new leaves and flowering stems from buds spaced closely on the underground stems. In fact, it can be a problem to remove if it extends beyond the space you have allowed it, especially if it has crept under paving—its rhizomes are tough and extensive.

The flowers last about a month and set to produce bright red, eye-catching berries, so all in all it is value for money. There is a variety with pink-tinged flowers, called *rosea*, another which is double-flowered, 'Prolificans', one with longer stems, 'Fortin's Giant', and a fourth whose leaves are variegated yellow, 'Variegata'.

A mixture of all these would make interesting groundcover, and would certainly jazz up a difficult area under a large tree. It is also a good cottage garden herb, perhaps being allowed to run along a wall of the house facing east or west where sun is only likely for part of the day, or where there are climbers covering the house wall and providing shade beneath them—clematis and honeysuckle both grow vigorously enough for this purpose. Be sure that you want it there; it will be difficult to remove from amongst the roots of the climbers if you decide to do away with it.

Lily-of-the-valley does not need much care and attention; a good mulch of rotted organic matter at some time during the year, preferably in late autumn or late winter will encourage it. To keep up the flower quality and quantity, replants are needed every few years by division of the underground stems in early autumn, spacing them about 15 cm (6 in) apart.

Sweet violet

Another small plant with a penetrating and individual fragrance which is also said to like shade, is *Viola odorata*. The dog violet, *V. canina*, is always found in light woodland—it is a pity it is not scented. The sweet violet grows wild in much more open places, such as sunny banks, at the foot of ledges, beside sunny paths and tracks and so on, generally where there is much more sun than shade. What it must have, however, is moist humus, preferably a well-drained soil; bad drainage is a killer. Shade for most of the time cuts down its flowering and results in a leafy mass, good for groundcover but rather boring otherwise.

Flowering is in spring and can last for up to two months if the spring is cool. In an early season, the flowers may open in mid winter and continue to do so intermittently until quite well on in spring, and there is a variety called *praecox*, which naturally starts to flower even earlier, in mid autumn, and goes on through the winter until early spring, just as strongly scented as the species, and its white form, *V. o. alba*.

Violets extend themselves by runners like strawberries, rooting plantlets at the end of stems and then lengthening the stem again, but spread is not as fast or extensive as the strawberry. Moreover, as the patch enlarges, the centre can become bare, unless the plants are kept mulched with rotted garden compost or similar organic material.

Violets have been cultivated for the sake of their perfume for many centuries, though this was not just used as a pleasing smell by the Greeks and Romans. It was thought to be the equivalent of the modern aspirin in chasing away headaches and could be used by insomniacs to encourage a good night's sleep. In Gerard's time, they were made into 'garlands for the head, nosegaies and poesies, which are delightful to look on and pleasant to smell too'. He described white violets, and double forms of both colours, still available today with the exception of the white double, which does not seem to be around now.

Violets have also been much used in food, mainly as crystallized flowers to decorate cakes, trifles and puddings, when they provide a unique, sweet and scented flavour of their own. Their other uses have included addition to or being the main constituent of jellies, salads, jams, a medicinal syrup, mousse, vinegar, tea, cake, butter, icecream, marzipan, a variety of summer drinks, soufflés and wine (popular with the Romans).

Violets can be grown in an average sort of way without difficulty, but a little care and attention provides a profusion of flowers, larger, more scented and for a longer period. Planting should be in early–mid spring, about 30 cm (1 ft) apart, using rooted runners for preference. Alternatively old plants can be divided, as soon after flowering as possible, allowing each division to have three crowns, and planting at once. Water in and keep well watered if the weather is dry, and protect from hot summer sun if natural shade is not available—for example, cover the plants with flower pots in the middle of the day.

Choose a place where they receive sun and shade at some time during the day, beneath roses, round climbers where there are tall perennial plants nearby, in a west- or east-facing rock border, at the foot of pergolas and arches, and round or beneath shrubs whose top growth is light and well above the soil. They will grow in practically any soil, but thrive in moist, well broken down, heavy types, or deep sandy ones, and in both cases plenty of rotted organic matter should be forked in well before planting.

Mulch after flowering, either with crumbly garden compost or peat, or with a mixture of peat and sand, and remove the runners as the summer progresses—the clumps of leaves will enlarge sufficiently on their own to cover the soil, and have the merit of being evergreen. You can leave the runners attached, but the plants tend to become thin in the middle, and flowering is less good.

Watch for violet mite, which infests the leaves and makes them thick and blistered; remove at once as soon as you see any at all. Red spider mite can be another problem, but only if the wrong position is chosen, i.e. too hot, sunny or dry.

Rosemary

Rosemary does not seem to be a likely plant for a groundcover, but there is a form called *Rosmarinus lavandulaceus* (syn. *R. officinalis prostratus*), which lies along the soil surface. Its habit of growth is trailing, and it forms thick mats of its aromatic foliage in time, covered with blue flowers in spring. It is much more tender than the upright forms, and will need a sunny mild garden, mainly free of frost, but given that and a light soil, it will grow well and cover rocky or stony ground particularly satisfactorily.

CHAPTER NINE

PLANT GROWTH AND HEALTH

There are some golden rules which are common to the good growth and health of plants, regardless of the type of plant, whether it is a shrub, herbaceous perennial, annual or herb. They are quite simple, but if not followed, plants may not thrive after being planted, or if they do take hold and grow, they never grow at their best.

THE SOIL

It all starts with the soil; feed the soil, not the plants. In other words, regularly at some time every year, dress with rotted organic matter such as garden compost, peat, farm manure of some kind, spent mushroom compost, leafmould, straw (it must be rotted), spent hops and so on. Dig it in before planting, or use it as a mulch, covering the soil round the plants, as thick as you can manage, and blanketing as large an area as possible.

If the soil is sandy, stony, shingly, or chalky, use a concentrated fertilizer as well, such as organic Growmore, blood-fish-and-bone or dried and powdered seaweed. If the planting is going to be dense, use it in this circumstance, too, and if after a year or so's planting, growth is not very good, use it in spring, sprinkled round the plants and forked in lightly, preferably just before rain. In time, with the constant addition of organic matter, extra food of this kind should not be necessary.

CHOICE OF SITE

Choose a position which gives the plant as near as possible the conditions it would have had in its natural habitat. If in doubt as to its needs, refer to a gardening encyclopaedia such as the RHS *Dictionary of Gardening* or Sanders' *Encyclopaedia of Gardening*. The plant's country of origin is usually supplied, if nothing else, and this will at least give a clue. Basic requirements can be for sun or shade, acid or alkaline soil, and dry or wet conditions for the roots; further refinements may be shelter from wind, freedom from frost, plenty of space and shade from midday sun.

Fig. 11 *Ways of protecting plants from wind and/or cold.*
    (a) Cover evergreen shrubs completely with a plastic sheet.
    (b) Make a wigwam of evergreen branches tied to three strong stakes for young trees.
    (c) Provide a wind shelter of plastic sheet or sacking for newly planted perennials.

PLANTING

Plant as quickly as possible; the longer the roots are unprotected by soil, or a soil-ball of roots is out of the ground, the more the plant's chances of survival become doubtful. Never expose the roots to the air, otherwise they dry up; this can happen extremely rapidly, so wrap them in plastic sheet to keep them moist. If ordered plants arrive dry, immerse them at once in a bucket of water for an hour or so.

Prepare the planting hole in advance some days or weeks earlier, by digging it out, forking up the base, and mixing rotted organic matter with the returned base. If it is not possible to do this in advance, do it at the time of planting.

Spread roots out completely in a planting hole which is bigger than necessary, or position a root-ball centrally in a hole which is also slightly too big. Fill it in with crumbly soil—use potting compost if the soil will not crumble, firm it in well, water the plant unless rain is imminent, and mulch the surface of the soil round it. Stake a tree well.

Plant bulbs at twice their own depth with a little sand at the base of the hole. Plant summer flowering varieties in spring, autumn flowering kinds in mid summer, and spring flowering bulbs and most lilies in autumn.

DEADHEADING

The repeated removal of dead flowers as soon as they have finished encourages the production of more, and lengthens the flowering period. It also prevents seed production, so if you want seedlings, leave the flowers on the plant. If flowers are wanted for pot pourri, they should be cut just after they open fully, on a dry day early in the morning.

PRUNING

Shrubs, roses and climbers are the types of plants which require cutting regularly to keep their growth at its most floriferous and attractive. All should have dead shoots removed, otherwise they clutter the plant up, prevent air and light getting into it and provide a source from which pests and diseases can spread. Recognize them by the brown, not green stem, lack of leaf or withered leaves, and no flowers. Cut back to green bark, just above a living shoot or bud.

Shoots which are small, thin and weak, which grow into the centre of the plant, or jostle one another, should be removed completely for the same reasons; this general pruning is best done in spring, just as new leaves are starting to unfold.

If you are dealing with shrubs, remember there are two types: spring- and early summer-flowering, and mid summer- to autumn-flowering. Winter-flowering types are regarded as spring-flowering for this purpose, but generally hardly need any special pruning.

Spring- and early summer-flowering varieties should be pruned directly their flowers have finished, by cutting off completely the flowered shoots, back to a point just above a strong new shoot. It will be on this year's new shoots that flowers will appear next year.

Mid summer- to autumn-flowering shrubs should be pruned in early to mid spring, again cutting off flowered growth, which will be last year's shoots. New shoots will grow to take their place, and it will be on these that this type of shrub

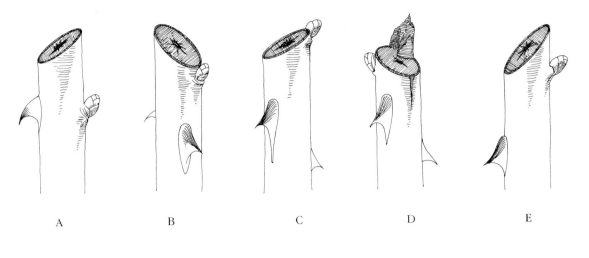

A   B   C   D   E

Fig. 12 *Right and wrong pruning cuts:*
    (a) *Too far from bud*
    (b) *Cut angled wrong way*
    (c) *Too close to bud*
    (d) *Cut ragged and torn*
    (e) *Correct cut*

will flower in the new season.

There are exceptions to these general rules but not many, and with experience, it is possible to tailor one's approach to the pruning of a particular shrub to get the best out of it. Try to keep the natural shape as far as possible.

Pruning of climbing plants of the woody kind is mostly a case of keeping them within the space allotted to them. Some cutting back will probably be necessary during the growing season, together with some tying in, otherwise follow the principles which apply to shrubs in general. Late summer-flowering kinds of clematis can be left unpruned, to form a tangled mass of flowers and leaves, with occasional hard cutting back in some years, or cut back hard every year, to about 90 cm (3 ft) above the ground.

WATERING

Plants should never reach the stage when they are visibly wilting; by then irreversible damage will have been done and, even if they are not actually killed through lack of water, they will have been weakened, and some of the roots will have died. When a dry period continues for more than five days, particularly in hot weather, and unless the soil is really damp, as it may be if heavy, give a good prolonged watering in the evening with a sprinkler, and repeat this every few days until rain occurs. Plants which grow close to walls or fences, or under trees, are particularly vulnerable, and need even closer watching. Mulching in spring will help to keep soil moist.

PEST AND DISEASE CONTROL

Since most sprays smell unpleasant, and the object of growing fragrant plants is self-evident, the answer is, do not spray! If you refrain from using any pesticides at all, the natural predators and parasites will build up to do your pest control for you . Fungus diseases are a different problem, but if plants get this kind of infection it usually means that either they are planted in the wrong place, or are not being treated in the way they need. Many roses are resistant to such diseases as black spot and mildew, but if they are badly infected every year, it would be better to dispense with them and grow alternatives that do not succumb. Sometimes the weather encourages spread of diseases, and it is often true that diseases spread, especially mildew, towards the end of the growing season, when plants are less vigorous and beginning the count-down to winter dormancy.

If you feel that some sort of spray is essential, use the safest one such as soft soap, pyrethrum and its analogues, sulphur, copper and biological controls.

PROPAGATION

There are various ways of multiplying plants, all of them easy, though some are less easy than others. The two easiest are the division method, and the splitting-off method. *Division* is merely a matter of breaking a plant into several pieces and using all but the central section. It mainly applies to soft-stemmed perennials, both herbaceous border plants and herbs.

Splitting-off can involve removal of small bulbs from the parent bulb and growing them on to flowering size; taking suckers which have originated from the roots of the parent plant, but have come up some distance from it, and using plantlets on runners.

Layering is another easy method, and some plants do it without help. When a stem is close enough to the ground to touch it, roots appear on the underside at that point; thyme will do this, and so will pinks and carnations. Otherwise it is a case of using low-growing stems, making a slanting cut on the underside partially through the stem opposite a leaf joint, and pinning the stem down on to the soil on either side of the cut.

Cuttings are a third method of vegetative increase, which will provide an exact copy of the parent plant. There are three kinds: soft, semi-hardwood, and hardwood. Of the three, the last-named is the easiest in which to initiate roots, and is used for hard-wooded plants such as shrubs, climbers and some roses. In mid–late autumn use a length of new shoot about 30 cm (12 in) long, whose bark has turned brown, make a clean cut at the base, and cut the tip off. Remove the leaves if they have not already fallen, put it in the ground outdoors to a depth of three-quarters of its length, with a little sand at the base of the hole, and firm it in well; choose a sheltered sunny place and mark it. Remove the rooted cutting to its permanent place the following autumn.

Semi-hardwood cuttings are taken from mid summer to early autumn, are about 7–15 cm (3–6 in) long, and have the end part of the stem brown and hard, the tip still soft and green. Such cuttings are put into compost in pots to half their length with their lower leaves removed, and put in a closed frame outdoors, or with a blown-up plastic bag secured round the rim of the pot. Rooting takes two to six weeks in most cases. Heel cuttings are not cut, but torn off the parent stem with a sliver of bark attached and thereby produce more roots.

Fig. 13 *Layering clematis*
  (a) *Remove leaf from 18-month-old shoot near ground*
  (b) *Make slanting cut on underside of stem opposite leaf joint, partially through stem*
  (c) *Peg cut stem down into compost with tip of shoot vertical*
  (d) *Cover stem with compost and support shoot tip with split cane*

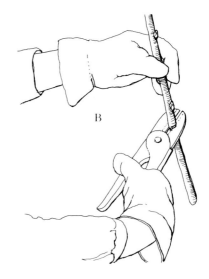

Fig. 14 *Making hardwood cuttings.*
   (a) *Cut off ripe new season's shoot in autumn.*
   (b) *Trim to about 12 in (30 cm) long, remove tip with slanting cut, and base just below a bud with a straight cut.*
   (c) *Make a slit trench outdoors in sheltered position, with a little sand at the bottom.*
   (d) *Insert cutting to three-quarters of its length and firm in.*
   (e) *Plant rooted cutting the following autumn in its permanent position.*

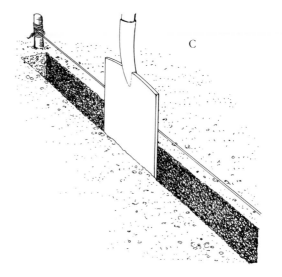

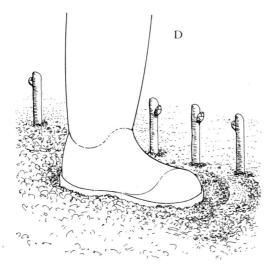

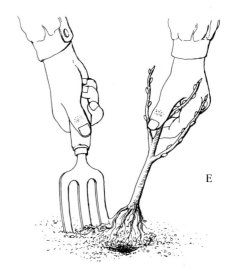

Soft cuttings consist of the tips of new young shoots, about 10 cm (4 in) long, again with the lower leaves removed, and buried for half their length in potting compost in a pot, protected with a plastic bag, or put into a closed propagator. Time to take is early–late summer, and rooting should be quick, in two to three weeks.

If you are growing from *seed*, whether in or outdoors, make sure that the soil or compost is always moist, and cover the seed to its own depth, except for fine, dust-like seed, which should not be covered. Sow either into compost, or into a soil with a fine crumbly structure. Germination is quickest in warm soil or compost, and when seed is freshly ripe. Best times to sow are in late summer–early autumn, or in spring.

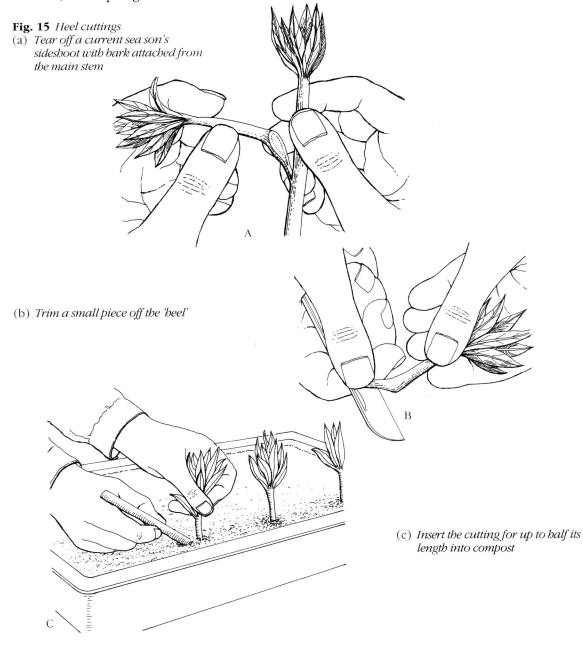

Fig. 15 *Heel cuttings*
(a) *Tear off a current season's sideshoot with bark attached from the main stem*

(b) *Trim a small piece off the 'heel'*

(c) *Insert the cutting for up to half its length into compost*

INDEX

Abelia chinensis, 62
Absinthe, 107
Achillea millefolium, 114–15
Acorus calamus, 22, 105
Alecost, 108
Almond aroma, 12
Aminoid odour group, 13
Anethum graveolens, 102
Animal-scented aroma group, 13
Aniseed aroma, 12
Annuals, 41–48
Aquilegia fragrans, 30
    vulgaris, 30
Arabs, perfume and, 15, 22
Aroma, groups, 11–13
    for protection, 10
    substance of, 10–11
Aromatherapy, 20
Artemisia abrotanum, 106–7
    absinthium, 107
Asperula odorata, 115
Asphodeline lutea, 52
Asphodelus fistulosus, 52
    ramosus, 52
Attar of roses, 80
Auricula, 31
Azalea, 57

Balm of Gilead, 19, 103–4
Balsam poplar, 79
Balsamita major, 108
Bark, aromatic, 13, 78–79
Bees, pollination by, 9
Beetles, pollination by, 9
Bergamot, 49
Biennials, 28–30, 49
Birds, pollination by, 9
Bog myrtle, 79
Bowellia carteri, 19
Bottlebrush, 78
Bourbon roses, 84–86
Britain, perfume and, 23–24

Broom, 66
Buddleia davidii, 62–63
    fallowiana, 63
Bulbs, planting, 120
    spring, 31
    summer, 33–34, 38–40
Burning bush, 10, 50
Butterflies, pollination by, 9
Butterfly bush, 62–63

Californian allspice, 63–64
Callistemon citrinus, 78
Calycanthus occidentalis, 63–64
Camellia sasanqua, 71
Camphor aroma group, 13
    plant, 108
Campion, 49
Carnation, 34–37
Catchfly, 49
Catnep, 108
Cedronella triphylla, 19, 103–4
Centaurea montana, 30
Cerastium tomentosum, 98
Chamaemelum nobile, 114
Chamomile, 114
Cheiranthus cheiri, 28–30
Cherry pie, 44
Chimonanthus praecox, 71–74
Chionanthus retusus, 65
    virginicus, 65
Chlorophyll, 8–9
Choisya ternata, 54–56
Chrysanthemum balsamita, 108
Cistus × *cyprius*, 78
    × *ladanifer*, 78
    laurifolius, 79
Clematis cirrhosa, 76–78
    flammula, 78
    rehderiana, 78
Clerodendrum bungei, 64
    fragrans, 64
    trichotomum, 64

Clove aroma, 12
Colour, perfume and, 8–9
Commiphora myrrha, 18–19
    opobalsamum, 19, 103
Convallaria majalis, 116
Corms, spring, 31
    summer, 38–40
Corsican mint, 114
Costmary, 108
Cowslip, 31
Crinum bulbispermum, 40
    × *powelli*, 40
Crocus sativus, 21
Curry plant, 104
Cuttings, 122–5
Cyclamen repandum, 31
Cytisus battandieri, 65–66

Daphne mezereum, 74
Daylily, 38
Deadheading, 120
Dianthus caryophyllus, 34–35
    plumarius, 36
Dictamnus albus, 10, 50
Dill, 102
Diseases, 122
Distillation of perfume, 15
Division, 122

Eglantine, 90
Egyptians, perfume and, 18, 19–20
Elaeagnus commutata, 56
Elder, 102
Embalming, 20
Enfleurage, 15
Eucalyptus aroma group, 13
Eucalyptus globulus, 79
    gunnii, 79
Europe, perfume and, 22–24
Evening primrose, 49
Expression of perfume, 17
Extraction of perfume, 15–17

Fennel, 102
Feverfew, 107–8
Flower perfume groups, 11–13
Foeniculum vulgare, 102
Foliage, aromatic *see* Leaves, aromatic
Fragrance *see* Perfume
Frankincense, 19
Fritillaria imperialis, 28
Fruit-scented perfume group, 12

Galtonia candicans, 34
Garden design history, 24
Genista aetnensis, 66
  hispanica, 66
Gladiolus, 40
Gorse, 61
Grasse, 25
Greeks, perfume and, 15, 20–21
Groundcovers, 115–17

Hamamelis mollis, 74
  virginiana, 74
Helichrysum angustifolium, 104
Heliotropium peruvianum, 44
Hemerocallis lutea, 38
Herb(s), aromas, 26
  culinary, 98–103
  gardens, 109–11
  household, 103–9
  lawns, 112–15
Hesperis matronalis, 33
Honey perfume group, 12
  water, 22
Honeysuckle, 69–70, 78
Hungary water, 22
Hyacinth, 31
  South African summer, 34
Hyssopus officinalis, 106

Iberis amara, 41
Indians, perfume and, 18
Indole, 12
Indoloid aroma group, 12–13
Insect pollination, 90
Iris 'Florentina', 27–28
  pallida, 28
  reticulata, 27

Jasminum, 70–71
  officinale, 71
  revolutum, 71
Jonquil, 31

Knot garden, 109
Kyphi, 19

Labdanum, 22
Laburnum, 56–57
  alpinum, 56
  × *watereri* 'Vossii', 56
Lathyrus odoratus, 47–48
Laurus nobilis, 102
Lavender, 25, 26, 109
Lavender cotton, 106
Lavandula angustifolia, 109
  stoechas, 109
Lawns, herbal, 112–15
Layering, 122
Leaf aroma, 10, 78–79
  groups, 13
  rose, 90–91
Lemon balm, 103
Lemon perfume group, 12
Ligusticum officinalis, 100
Ligustrum ovalifolium, 64
Lilac, 60
Lilium auratum, 38–40
  candidum, 38
  regale, 40
Lily, 38–40
Lily-of-the-valley, 116
Lime, 67
Liquid perfumes, 21–22
Lonicera fragrantissima, 78
  periclymenum, 69–70
Lotus, 19
Lovage, 100

Maceration, 17
Magnolia, 66–67
  delavayi, 66
  grandiflora, 66
  hypoleuca, 66
  stellata, 57
Mahonia 'Charity', 75–76
  japonica, 75
Marjoram, 102–3
Matthiola bicornis, 44
  incana, 44
Melissa officinalis, 103
Mentha × *gentilis*, 99
  × *piperita*, 98, 99
  pulegium, 113
  requienii, 114
Mexican orange blossom, 54–56
Mezereon, 74
Middle Ages, perfume in, 22

Mignonette, 48
Mint, 89–99, 114
  aroma group, 13
Mock-orange blossom, 69
Monarda citriodora, 49
  didyma, 49–50
Moringa aptera, 22
Moss rose, 86
Moths, pollination by, 9
Musk rose, 86–87
Myrica gale, 79
Myrrh, 18–19
Myrrhis odorata, 104
Myrtus communis, 67

Narcissus jonquilla, 31
  minor, 31
  odorus regulosus, 31
  rupicola, 31
Nardostachys jatamansii, 19
Nelumbo nucifera, 19
Nemesia, 41
Nepeta cataria, 108
Nocotiana, 41
Normans, perfume and, 22

Odour *see* Perfume *or* Aroma
Oenothera biennis, 49
Oil of ben, 22
Oils, essential, 10–11
Ointments, 21–22
Origanum onites, 102
  vulgare, 102–3

Pelargoniums, scented-leaved, 52–53
Pennyroyal, 113
Peony, 30–31
Perennials, 49–50
Perfume extraction, 15–17
  groups, 11–13
  history of, 18–25
  pollination and, 8–9
  substance of, 10–11
Persians, perfume and, 20
Pests, 122
Petunia, 41
Philadelphus, 69
  coronarius, 69
Phlox, 50–52
Pinks, 34–37
Pittosporum, 57
Planting, 120
Pollination of plants, 8–9

Polyanthus, 31
Populus trichocarpa, 79
Powdered perfumes, 21–22
Primula, 30–31
   veris, 31
Privet, 64
Propagation, 122–5
Pruning, 120–1

Reseda odorata, 48
Rhododendron luteum, 57
Rock rose, 78–79
Romans, perfume and, 15, 21
Rosa alba, 81
   banksiae alba, 89
   b. 'Kiftsgate', 89
   centifolia, 83–84, 86
   damascena, 81
   eglanteria, 90
   gallica, 83
   gigantea, 89
   moschata, 86–87
   odorata 'Ochroleuca', 89
   o. 'Odorata', 89
Rose, Bourbon, 84–86
   climbing, 89–90, 96–97
   cultivation, 97
   floribunda, 94
   history, 21, 80–81
   hybrid tea, 94
   modern, 91–97
   moss, 86
   musk, 86–87
   old, 81–91
   patio, 96
   perfume group, 11
   plants to grow with, 91
Rose-water, 80
Rosemary, 99, 117
Rosemarinus lavandulaceus, 117
   officinalis, 99
Rue, 91, 105–6

Rushes, scented, 22
Ruta graveolens, 105–6

Saffron crocus, 21
Sage, 100–2
Salvia, 91
   angustifolia, 100
   officinalis, 100
Sambucus nigra, 102
Santolina chamaecyparissus, 106
Sarcococca confusa, 76
Saturja, 100
Savory, 100
Sea campion, 49
Seeds, 125
Shrubs, autumn/winter-flowering,
   71–78
   spring-flowering, 54–61
   summer/autumn-flowering,
   62–71
Silene, 49
Silver berry, 56
Siting plants, 118
Skimmia × *rogersii*, 60
   japonica, 57–60
Snow-in-summer, 98
Soils, 118
Southernwood, 106–7
Spikenard, 19
Splitting-off, 122
Sulphur aroma group, 13
Sweetbriar, 90–91
Sweet bay, 102
   box, 76
   cicely, 104
   flag, 105
   pea, 47
   rocket, 33
   violet, 116–17
   woodruff, 115
Syringa, 60
   meyeri, 60

   × *persica*, 60
   sweginzowii, 60
   vulgaris, 60
   see also Philadelphus

Tanacetum balsamita, 108
   parthenium, 107–8
   vulgare, 108
Tansy, 108
Terpenes, 10–11
Thyme, 99–100
   for lawns, 112–13
Thymus caespititus, 113
   × *citriodorus*, 99–100
   herba-barona, 113
   serpyllum, 112–13
   vulgaris, 99–100
Tilia × *euchlora*, 67
Trees, spring-flowering, 54–61
   summer/autumn-flowering,
   62–71
Turpentine aroma group, 13

Ulex europaeus, 61
   minor, 61
Unguents, 22

Vanilla aroma, 12
Verbena, 47
Viburnum × *bodnantense*, 76
   farreri, 76
   'Park Farm', 76
Viola odorata, 33, 116–17
Violet, 116–17
   perfume group, 11

Wallflower, 28–30
Watering, 121
Winter sweet, 71–74
Witch-hazel, 74

Yarrow, 114–15